THE CAMINO INGLÉS AND RUTA DO MAR

About the Authors

Laura Perazzoli lives and works in Portland, Oregon. She completed her first pilgrimage in 2004 on the Camino Francés. After this trip, she was excited to provide others with a similar experience and has since led student pilgrimage trips on the Camino Francés, the Camino del Norte and Primitivo, the Via Francigena and Le Puy route in France. Laura first walked the Camino del Norte and Primitivo in 2009 and has since walked these routes three additional times to ensure up-to-date route information for this guidebook.

Dave Whitson is a high-school History teacher in Portland, Oregon. He made his first pilgrimage in 2002 on the Camino Francés and was inspired to return with a group of his high-school students, which he did in 2004. He has led a total of 15 student pilgrimage trips and completed many others independently. Dave first walked the Camino del Norte and Camino Primitivo in 2008 and has subsequently returned on six other occasions.

THE CAMINO INGLÉS AND RUTA DO MAR

TO SANTIAGO DE COMPOSTELA AND FINISTERRE FROM FERROL, A CORUÑA OR RIBADEO

by Dave Whitson and Laura Perazzoli

JUNIPER HOUSE, MURLEY MOSS,
OXENHOLME ROAD, KENDAL, CUMBRIA LA9 7RL
www.cicerone.co.uk

© Dave Whitson and Laura Perazzoli 2019
Third edition 2019
ISBN: 978 1 78631 006 4

Replaces *The Northern Caminos* (ISBN: 978 1 85284 794 4), together with companion volume *The Camino del Norte and Primitivo* (ISBN: 978 1 78631 014 9)

Printed in China on behalf of Latitude Press Ltd

A catalogue record for this book is available from the British Library.

Route mapping by Lovell Johns www.lovelljohns.com
All photographs are by the authors unless otherwise stated.
Contains OpenStreetMap.org data © OpenStreetMap contributors, CC-BY-SA.

NASA relief data courtesy of ESRI

Updates to this Guide

While every effort is made by our authors to ensure the accuracy of guidebooks as they go to print, changes can occur during the lifetime of an edition. Any updates that we know of for this guide will be on the Cicerone website (www.cicerone.co.uk/1006/updates), so please check before planning your trip. We also advise that you check information about such things as transport, accommodation and shops locally. Even rights of way can be altered over time. We are always grateful for information about any discrepancies between a guidebook and the facts on the ground, sent by email to updates@cicerone.co.uk or by post to Cicerone, Juniper House, Murley Moss, Oxenholme Road, Kendal LA9 7RL, United Kingdom.

Register your book: To sign up to receive free updates, special offers and GPX files where available, register your book at www.cicerone.co.uk.

Front cover: Near Calle de Poulo (Inglés, Stage 4)

CONTENTS

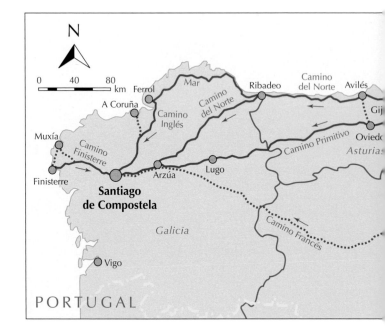

Pontedeume (Inglés, Stage 1)

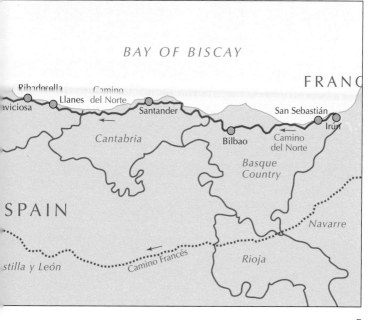

BAY OF BISCAY

FRANC

Ribadesella

Camino
del Norte

Llanes

aviciosa

Santander

San Sebastián

Irún

Cantabria

Bilbao

Camino
del Norte

Basque
Country

SPAIN

Navarre

Camino Francés

Rioja

stilla y León

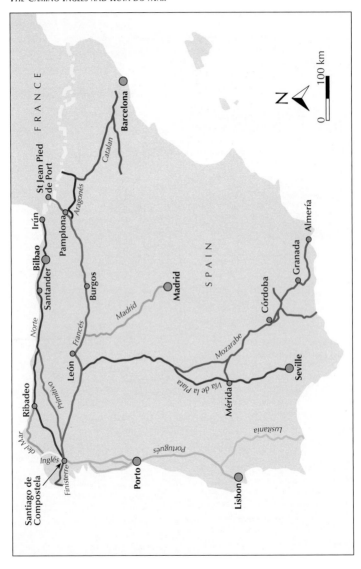

Symbols used on route maps

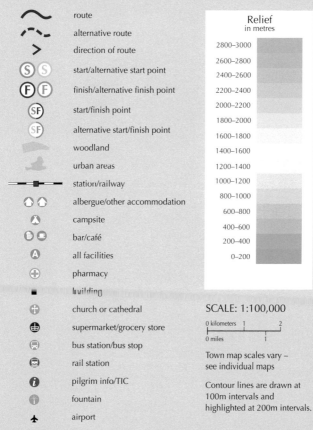

		Relief in metres
~	route	2800–3000
⌐⌐⌐	alternative route	2600–2800
>	direction of route	2400–2600
Ⓢ Ⓢ	start/alternative start point	2200–2400
Ⓕ Ⓕ	finish/alternative finish point	2000–2200
ⓈⒻ	start/finish point	1800–2000
ⓈⒻ	alternative start/finish point	1600–1800
	woodland	1400–1600
	urban areas	1200–1400
▬■▬	station/railway	1000–1200
⌂ ⌂	albergue/other accommodation	800–1000
⌂	campsite	600–800
⊕ ⊕	bar/café	400–600
Ⓐ	all facilities	200–400
⊕	pharmacy	0–200
■	building	
✚	church or cathedral	
⊕	supermarket/grocery store	
⊞	bus station/bus stop	
⊞	rail station	
𝒊	pilgrim info/TIC	
●	fountain	
✈	airport	

SCALE: 1:100,000

0 kilometers 1 2
0 miles 1

Town map scales vary – see individual maps

Contour lines are drawn at 100m intervals and highlighted at 200m intervals.

GPX files
GPX files for all routes can be downloaded for free at www.cicerone.co.uk//1006/GPX

Santiago Peregrino, atop the cathedral in Santiago de Compostela

ROUTE SUMMARY TABLES

Camino Inglés					
Stage	Start	Distance	Total ascent	Total descent	Page
1	Ferrol	29.5km	457m	457m	36
2	Pontedeume	20.7km	563m	537m	44
3	Betanzos	25.7km	749m	384m	50
4	Hospital de Bruma	24.7km	273m	437m	55
5	Sigüeiro	16.2km	264m	238m	60
Total	**Santiago de Compostela**	**116.8km**	**2306m**	**2053m**	
	Alternative start at A Coruña	33.6km	902m	528m	66

Ruta do Mar					
Stage	Start	Distance	Total ascent	Total descent	Page
1	Ribadeo	17.8km	149m	178m	76
2	Praia das Catedrais	21.8km	357m	369m	80
3	Foz	32.8km	538m	532m	88
4	San Cibrao	29.7km	832m	833m	96
5	Viveiro	31.2km	1054m	1052m	102
6	Cuiña	20.9km	669m	542m	110
7	Teixido	36.4km	918m	1057m	116
Total	**Xubia**	**190.6km**	**4517m**	**4563m**	

Camino Finisterre					
Stage	Start	Distance	Total ascent	Total descent	Page
1	Santiago de Compostela	20.5	501	592	129
2	Negreira	34.1	601	492	132
3	Olveiroa	32.2	468	728	135
Total	**Finisterre**	**86.8km**	**1570m**	**1872m**	
	Muxía extension	52.7	991	1334	138

The camino after Betanzos (Inglés, Stage 3)

INTRODUCTION

The rain in Spain falls mainly in Galicia, making the Iberian Peninsula's northwest corner a lush and verdant outdoor lover's paradise. Blessed with richly forested lands, rippling hills crisscrossed with gurgling creeks, and medieval stone villages nestled snugly in their midst, Galicia would be a desirable destination for walkers even if it were bereft of any historical or cultural significance. Of course, just the opposite is true; Galicia is home to one of the great pilgrimage sites in the world, Santiago de Compostela, and the most famous branch of the Camino de Santiago, the Camino Francés, draws nearly 200,000 pilgrims annually, with many pilgrims continuing onward to the coast of Finisterre and Muxía.

While the scenery of the Galician portion of the Camino Francés is stunning, it can be challenging for some to fully enjoy this walk due to the surging pilgrim traffic. Those seeking the best of both worlds – Galician grandeur and peaceful, contemplative walking conditions – have been drawn in recent years to the Camino Inglés, a much shorter pilgrimage that originates on the northern coast, either in Ferrol or A Coruña. The Inglés, so called because it was popular with pilgrims traveling via boat from the British Isles, offers many of the same qualities that make the Francés so popular, including reliable waymarking, consistent pilgrim hostels, and the opportunity to earn the Compostela in Santiago, a certificate that confirms and commemorates your pilgrimage.

For those seeking even greater solitude and sublimity, and possessing an adventurous streak to match, look to the Galician coast between Ribadeo, where the Camino del Norte turns inland, and Ferrol, where the Inglés begins. Over the last two decades, historians have diligently revealed the pilgrim roads that wound through this stunning terrain in the Middle Ages, providing an alternative approach to Santiago that passes through San Martiño de Mondoñedo, likely the oldest cathedral in Spain, and Viveiro, one of Galicia's most important ports. It also integrates another major pilgrimage site, San Andrés de Teixido, before joining the Inglés. While not yet recognized by the archbishopric of Santiago as an 'official' camino, and lacking the pilgrim infrastructure of those peer routes as a consequence, it offers some of the most striking and memorable scenery of any camino in Galicia, with dramatic cliffs, idyllic beaches, and evocative Romanesque shrines.

The majority of pilgrims begin their walk on the Camino Inglés in Ferrol; the route spans 116km and takes four to six days to complete. Alternatively, it is possible to initiate the Inglés in A Coruña, in which case the walk covers 75km. Distances on the Ruta do Mar are not as tidy, as there are many variants that allow for customization. Our recommended approach between Ribadeo and Xubia (near Ferrol on the Camino Inglés) runs 190km, but we include roughly 400km of routes to combine in crafting your adventure. Finally, the 87km continuation to Finisterre after Santiago is generally handled in three days, with an optional fourth-day extension to Muxía.

THE STORY OF SAINT JAMES

While countless pilgrimage shrines exist within the Catholic world, three cities stand out as major centers of pilgrimage. Two are obvious: Jerusalem is intimately associated with the life of Jesus, while Rome houses the relics of saints Peter and Paul, not to mention Saint Peter's Basilica. The third center, situated in an otherwise forgotten corner of Spain, is much more surprising. Santiago de Compostela, in Spain's northwestern region of Galicia, has a history built on equal parts rumor and legend.

Of Jesus's 12 apostles, perhaps less is known about Saint James (or Santiago) than any other. The brother of John and the son of an assertive mother, James is known for his temper and for being one of Jesus's first followers – and the first to be martyred. However, mystery surrounds James's

Santiago de Compostela's cathedral (Inglés, Stage 5)

life between the crucifixion of Christ and his own death. Spanish legend asserts that he brought the good word to the Iberian Peninsula, but with minimal success, winning very few followers. That said, on his subsequent return to the Holy Land he fared worse; he was decapitated by Herod Agrippa in AD44.

After James's death, the story goes, his disciples smuggled his body to the coast, where it was placed on a stone boat – lacking sails, oars, and sailors – and put to sea. Amazingly, and perhaps under the guidance of angels, this boat maneuvered westward across the Mediterranean and north into the Atlantic, before ultimately making landfall at Padrón on the Galician coast. Once there, two disciples met the boat, took James's body, and eventually buried him in present-day Santiago de Compostela. And then, almost eight centuries passed.

In 813, the hermit Pelayo had a vision in which a star shined brightly on a nearby field. Digging there, Pelayo made a stunning discovery: the very bones of Saint James, buried and forgotten so many years earlier. The timing couldn't have been better for the local Christians. With the Moorish conquest of the Iberian Peninsula nearly complete, their armies enjoying victory after victory behind the 'arm of Mohammed', the Christian Kingdom of Asturias in northern Spain was in dire straits. However, according to legend, the

Iglesia de Santa María, Neda (Inglés, Stage 1)

tide turned at the pivotal Battle of Clavijo. As the Asturian army prepared to face the much larger Muslim force, Saint James appeared before them on his white horse and led them into battle. So began the legend of Santiago Matamoros ('Saint James the Moorkiller'), one of the saint's two faces along the camino. In the other, Santiago Peregrino, his pilgrim identity, Saint James generally appears with a staff and scallop shell.

The cult of Santiago grew gradually over the next two centuries, before two major developments in the 12th century propelled Compostela to the forefront of the Christian world. First, Diego Gelmírez became the bishop of Santiago in 1101 (and archbishop in 1120), and quickly devoted his life to the aggrandizement of Compostela. Second, the 'Codex Calixtinus' emerged sometime in the 1130s. The first 'guidebook' to the Camino de Santiago, it included, among other things, a list of miracles attributed to Saint James, the history of the route, and a collection of practical advice for travelers, including warnings about 'evil toll gatherers' and the 'barbarous' locals.

At its peak in the Middle Ages, hundreds of thousands of pilgrims from all across Europe made the journey to Santiago de Compostela. After a decline following the Reformation and a near-total collapse in numbers during the Enlightenment period, the Camino de Santiago returned to prominence in the late 20th century.

A cruceiro near Foz (Ruta do Mar, Stage 3)

THE CAMINO INGLÉS AND RUTA DO MAR: YESTERDAY AND TODAY

While the Camino Francés enjoys greater prominence today than the many other routes to Santiago, that should not suggest that these other approaches through Galicia lack historical significance. Indeed, many pilgrims – most famously British and Scandinavian, although Germans and French also came in large numbers – reached Galicia by boat, landing at various places along the northern Spanish coast. While Ferrol is the point of departure for most contemporary pilgrims, due largely to the Santiago archbishopric's arbitrary rule that pilgrims must walk 100km to earn the Compostela, it was an inconsequential port for medieval pilgrims, who instead were drawn overwhelmingly to A Coruña.

Medieval pilgrims to Santiago on the Camino Inglés would have, in most cases, experienced a trip reminiscent of many contemporary travelers working through an agency. They booked their sea journey with a merchant ship that also transported goods to Galicia. Their efficient itinerary would orchestrate a quick and orderly walk from A Coruña to Santiago and back, moving as a group and supported by a guide, before returning to their home country. Of course, unlike contemporary travelers, they had to worry about first Vikings and later pirates!

The Mar's history is not as thoroughly documented, but Galician historian Xoán Ramón Fernández Pacios has pieced together a compelling sketch. It is clear that pilgrims walked from Ribadeo to Viveiro,

following a fairly uniform route that led to the basilica of San Martiño de Mondoñedo, although they followed several different trajectories onward from Viveiro. Two options led inland, joining the Camino del Norte in Vilalba (believed by most historians to be the most popular approach) or passing through Mondoñedo on the Norte en route to Lugo on the Camino Primitivo. A third, however, continued near the coast to Ortigueira. From there, pilgrims could connect directly with the Camino Inglés or loop past the shrine of San Andrés de Teixido, which had emerged as a major pilgrimage site in its own right. Pilgrim hospitals existed in Ribadeo, San Martiño de Mondoñedo, Lieiro (just after San Cibrao), Celeiro, and Viveiro, and Fernández Pacios speculates that

A Coruña (Inglés, Alternative start)

The Faro Illa Pancha, north of Ribadeo (Ruta do Mar, Stage 1)

roughly 1000 pilgrims walked this route between the 16th and 18th centuries.

The Camino Inglés is a fully developed pilgrimage with all necessary infrastructure. It was the fifth most walked Camino de Santiago in 2017, with 11,321 pilgrims earning the Compostela after walking it. By contrast, the Ruta do Mar is largely unknown, and while it's impossible to gauge how many trailblazers are trekking its tracks at any given time, it can probably be counted on one or two hands. This is further complicated by the abundance of route options, and it's important to note that we employ 'Ruta do Mar' loosely as an umbrella term to include not only the historical pilgrimage route to Santiago but also two other walking routes. The first, the Camino Natural da Ruta do Cantábrico, or Camino Cantábrico as we refer to it in the route descriptions, is a contemporary, purpose-built walking route that follows the coastline between Ribadeo and Ladrido, near Ortigueira. When the Mar is roadbound, or stuck on a less scenic stretch toward the interior, the Cantábrico often offers a more enjoyable – if longer – alternative. Later on, the Mar overlaps or parallels the Camiño de Mañón a Santo André (San Andrés) de Teixido, both heading westward from Ponte do Porto and then southward to Xubia. As the Mar gains popularity, a more 'orthodox' route will emerge, but for now each pilgrim will likely take a slightly (or dramatically) different approach.

GALICIAN HISTORY AND CULTURE

The first permanent settlements in Galicia, circular hill forts or castros, developed around 2000BC and are particularly abundant on the initial stages of the Mar. Attributed to the region's Celtic, or Celtiberian, population, this is the foundation of Galician identity and culture. While Rome took control of Galicia in 19BC – giving the region its name, 'Gallaecia,' in the process – it was almost exclusively focused on establishing and controlling transportation lines, in order to extract mineral wealth.

Christianity didn't take root in Galicia until around the year 200, drawing more attention in its early years for potential heresies than sacred sites. The discovery of Santiago's remains in the ninth century launched the region into European prominence, of course, transforming it into one of the centers of the Catholic world following centuries of obscurity. After the Asturian king Alfonso II sponsored the construction of a shrine around James's remains in 899, Archbishop Diego Gelmírez initiated its replacement with a cathedral, while building the site's international reputation.

As the Reconquista came to an end, the locus of Spanish power shifted southward, away from Galicia and the rest of northern Spain. This, combined with the Protestant Reformation and related decline in the importance of pilgrimage, brought about several centuries of regression for Galicia, as it found itself pushed to the margins once more. A brief, but unwanted, return to the spotlight occurred in 1589, when Sir Francis Drake launched an assault on Galicia, in order to rid Santiago of a 'pernicious superstition.' While the attack failed, thanks to the heroic of efforts of A Coruña's Maria Pita, it spurred the archbishop to hide the sacred remains of Saint James; the new hiding place was so effective that the relics weren't relocated for nearly three centuries.

The British didn't only sail into Galicia for trade and pilgrimage; they also arrived during the Peninsular War to support Spanish forces against Napoleon. After some initial successes, the British army saw the tide turn dramatically in the winter of 1809. Led by Sir John Moore, the British raced westward across northern Spain, desperately trying to reach a naval evacuation site in the port of A Coruña. After a final, high stakes battle in the port that cost Moore his life, the bulk of the British army managed to escape. While the men were saved and Napoleon's attention was successfully distracted from southern Spain, this was nonetheless viewed as a military disaster for England.

The 20th century brought Galicia back to the national forefront in an unexpected way, with the emergence of Galicia's own Francisco Franco. Born in Ferrol, the starting point of the Camino Inglés, Franco invested heavily in the promotion of tourism, and particularly by drawing attention to the Camino de Santiago. Eucalyptus was also introduced to the region during the Franco era. Given the rainy climate, it was believed that eucalyptus forests would thrive. And they have – perhaps too much – and now threaten many native species; there is an almost eerie quality to the absolute quiet that reigns within them.

Franco's death coincided with a resurgent nationalism among Galegos. The local language, Gallego, is immediately noticeable upon arrival in the region; note that the pilgrimage, for example, is now identified as the 'Camiño' de Santiago. Gallego is often described as a middle ground between Spanish and Portuguese. Those comfortable with either language will have no trouble communicating here (see Appendix B for a list of useful words).

CHOOSING YOUR CAMINO

The Camino Inglés is an ideal 'starter camino,' particularly for those who have time constraints or concerns about committing to a longer trek. The terrain is gentle enough to be manageable for all walkers (although certainly not flat!), stages can be kept relatively short, and there are some distinctly Galician towns to stay in offering lively experiences.

By contrast, the Ruta do Mar is best pursued, for now at least, by experienced walkers who can manage with far less reliable waymarking and more erratic facilities. Lacking

Pontedeume (Inglés, Stage 1)

albergues, it's a more expensive walk, and it can be a lonely experience. That said, it can also be a genuinely exciting process, being at the forefront of the recovery of a historic pilgrimage route. Ever wonder what it was like, walking the Camino Francés in the 1980s? Try the Mar now.

The most exciting part about the Mar's addition to the camino network is the potential to combine it with other routes. Pilgrims on the Camino del Norte, in particular, may be intrigued by the possibility of following the coast all the way to Ferrol, and then walking the Inglés into Santiago, avoiding the Camino Francés completely. This is a much longer walk, just over 300km if following our recommended approach, and exceeding the Norte/Francés combination by roughly 100km. However, it makes the pilgrimage a genuinely coastal experience nearly all the way to Santiago.

WHEN TO GO

Summer is the best time for both the Camino Inglés and the Ruta do Mar. Due to Galicia's climate, the off-season can be quite soggy, but the summer is consistently sunny and warm. On the Mar, more so than the Inglés, some of the towns are seasonal, thriving with beachgoers when the sun shines, but shutting down completely for the rest of the year. While there can be an accommodation crunch in late-July and August, this is generally not a concern beyond that.

That said, the off-season in Galicia has its charms. For those in search of solitude, it can be found along the Inglés in March or October, and almost all of the time on the Mar. Hotels that remain open can be talked into steep discounts. Indeed, both routes are viable year-round, although winter pilgrims should be prepared for wet and windy conditions.

PREPARATION AND PLANNING

The most important part of your preparation is the physical component, training for the rigors of the trail by doing some walking. The temptation might be strong with a shorter walk to skimp on training, but if you're transitioning from a more sedentary lifestyle it's still essential for enjoying a higher quality of life on the trail. Start slowly and build as your body allows, gradually increasing the distances covered. As you become stronger, add weight to your pack until its contents mirror what you will be carrying in Spain. If possible, hike on consecutive days; what might feel easy on fresh legs can be more draining on tired ones.

As you train, monitor three different areas. First, and most obvious, track how much distance you can cover comfortably, how your body responds to breaks, and what kinds of food provide you with the energy that you need. Second, keep a close eye on your feet, watching for blisters or other hot spots. Your goal here is to gradually build up calluses to help

The old mill of Molino de las Aceñas before Xubia (Inglés, Stage 1) (photo: Joe Williams)

prevent blistering on the camino. Third, test your gear and clothing, making sure that your pack fits properly, the weight is manageable, and your clothes don't chafe.

Read about the Camino de Santiago and pilgrimage in general before you go. Knowing some of the history and language of the region will add meaning to your walk. While the Camino Inglés lacks the proliferation of publications the Francés has enjoyed (and the Mar is all but ignored), some pilgrim journals have been published in recent years and can offer a useful preview of the experience (see Appendix C).

That said, unless your time schedule is quite restrictive, try to arrive in Spain without a rigid plan for your daily itinerary. Take it easy early on.

Many pilgrims arrive overflowing with energy and excitement, and go too far in their initial stages. It's better to stop too soon than push yourself too far, as the consequences of that exertion can linger in the forms of blisters, tendonitis, or other aches and pains.

BEING A PILGRIM

Making a trek as a pilgrim is a different experience in many ways from that involved in other lengthy walks. Several unique elements of the pilgrim experience are described below. Note that these are of particular relevance to the Camino Inglés, as the Mar doesn't have 'official' status as a camino from the Santiago archbishopric, though it is possible to gather stamps in places on the Mar.

Pilgrim passport

Known as the *credenciál* in Spanish, this document identifies you as a pilgrim. It is available in tourist offices in Ferrol and Ribadeo, from the pilgrim office in Santiago, and from many Camino-related groups, such as the Confraternity of Saint James (CSJ) in the UK (paid-up members only) and American Pilgrims in the US. You will get a stamp (sello) each day, usually in a pilgrim hostel, although it is also sometimes possible to get stamps in bars, churches, and town halls. For most pilgrims, this becomes a treasured memento of the journey, although it will have less relevance on the Mar.

The Compostela

Upon arrival in Santiago, the Archbishopric will award you the Compostela, a document acknowledging your completion of the pilgrimage, provided that you meet two conditions. First, you must have your credenciál, with stamps documenting your daily progress. Second, you must have walked from Ferrol on the Camino Inglés, taking care to get your first stamp in Ferrol. Alternatively, a recent rule change has made it possible to earn the Compostela walking the 75km from A Coruña, although it is more complicated. Pilgrims must complete the remaining 25km in their home country, on a spiritual walk that serves, in essence, as the beginning of their pilgrimage to Santiago. Evidence of this walk is required, perhaps through a series of stamps or a letter from the home parish. Confirm your plans with the pilgrim office in advance: oficinadelperegrino@catedraldesantiago.es.

Albergues

Your credenciál also gives you access to the pilgrim hostels (albergues de peregrino) on the Inglés. These provide dorm-style accommodation exclusively to pilgrims, and usually include facilities to wash both self and clothes. Some also offer kitchens. Pilgrims may spend only one night and are expected to leave by 0800 the next morning. The price for Galicia's municipal albergues is generally €6; private albergues cost more and may be open to non-pilgrims.

Pilgrim ethic

A popular saying in Spanish is *'Turistas manden; peregrinos agradecen'* ('Tourists demand; pilgrims give thanks'). While challenging to remember at the end of a long day, it is an important message to keep in mind. Albergues are typically run by voluntary hosts (*hospitaleros*). Often, they are backed by the financial support of the local community. Waymarks are maintained by local organizations. It is easy to find fault with many things along the way, but be cognizant of how many people are giving up their time, money, and energy to make your pilgrimage possible.

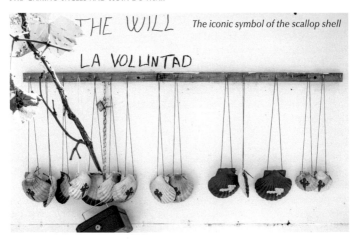

The iconic symbol of the scallop shell

GETTING THERE AND BACK

Camino Inglés: from A Coruña

By air
Vueling, Iberia, Air Europa, and TAP Portugal fly to A Coruña airport. From there, take the 4051 bus to the city center (every 30mins).

By train
RENFE offers frequent connections between A Coruña and Santiago de Compostela (30–40min, €6–7), five daily links between A Coruña and Ferrol (1¼hrs, €6–8), and long-distance services extending to Madrid and Barcelona.

By bus
MonBus operates hourly buses between A Coruña and Santiago de Compostela (1hr, €6–10) and five daily buses connecting Ferrol and Santiago (1¼hrs, €5–10). Arriva offers services between A Coruña and Ferrol (hourly, 1hr, €7). Once again, ALSA is the company of choice for long-distance connections.

Getting back from Santiago de Compostela

By air
Lavacolla airport, just outside of Santiago, is well connected with Spain and the rest of Europe, offering multiple routes operated by RyanAir (www.ryanair.com), EasyJet (www.easyjet.com), and Air Berlin (www.airberlin.com). Although Iberia sometimes advertises a special discounted fare for pilgrims with Compostelas, it's almost always cheaper to book in advance, if possible.

By train
RENFE runs six trains daily to Madrid (5–6hrs, €30–80). There is also a daily service from Santiago to Hendaye at the start of the Camino del Norte; from there, connections to Paris and other European towns are possible.

By bus
ALSA is once again the best bet.

EQUIPMENT

Remember that you will have to carry everything you take, every day. The guiding principle is to pack light, focusing on what is absolutely necessary and cutting out everything else. As the caminos pass regularly through towns, it will be possible to restock or acquire new supplies if it becomes necessary.

Walking through eucalyptus (Ruta do Mar, Stage 2)

Footwear
Walkers passionately debate whether shoes or boots are superior. Modern crosstrainers typically provide a great deal of support and comfort, without the weight and bulkiness of boots, and are advisable for most. If you do prefer to wear boots, make sure that they are broken in prior to departure. Outside of summer, it is worth considering water-proof shoes. In addition, bring a pair of sandals suitable for albergue showers and post-walk strolls around town.

Sleeping bag
Those walking in the summer who don't get cold too easily should consider bringing a sleep-sheet (sheet-sleeping bag). Silk liners weigh little and suffice for many. However, if you do not fit in those categories, a sleeping bag will be necessary. Look for an ultra-lightweight +5 degrees Celsius bag.

Rucksack
Pack size will be determined in large part by your sleeping bag decision. Those who opt for a sleep-sheet could walk the camino with a pack as small as 30 liters. With a sleeping bag, something in the 45 liter range will be needed. Regardless, a good fit is critical. Look for a pack that is properly sized for your torso and keeps the weight on your hips.

Clothing
Aim for two or three sets of clothes (shirt/top, socks, underwear) – one

or two in your pack and one on you – along with two pairs of pants (trousers)/shorts. Avoid cotton. Synthetic clothing wicks moisture from the body, dries quickly, and packs light. Finally, bring a warm outer layer. In the off-season, a long-sleeved/legged base layer is recommended as well.

Poncho

When walking in Galicia, and especially along the coast, be aware that the weather can be unpredictable. A good poncho will cover both person and pack and can be donned quickly. Otherwise, waterproof clothing and a rain cover for your pack will do. If you're walking outside of summer, you may prefer more extensive raingear.

Water

Personal preference will determine the choice of either a bottle or hydration bladder, but make sure to have at least one liter of water with you at all times, and more on certain stretches.

Pack towel

A synthetic, chamois-style towel packs lighter and smaller than a normal towel and dries faster.

Basic first-aid kit

Bring small amounts of most first-aid essentials; it's easy to buy more if you run out. Make sure to carry a good supply of footcare materials, including Compeed, moleskin or another similar product to cover blisters.

Flashlight/headlamp

Essential for late-night bathroom runs, early-morning packing, and pre-sunrise walking.

Toiletries

Limit these to the essentials.

Other gear worth considering

A hat, sunglasses, camp pillow, notepad/pen, eating utensils and bowl, digital camera, trekking poles, spare set of prescription spectacles, Spanish–English dictionary, and maps.

ACCOMMODATION

Albergues, providing dorm-style accommodation exclusively for pilgrims on a 'first-come, first-served basis', are available in eight towns on the Camino Inglés. Outside of summer, they can usually accommodate demand quite comfortably, but they can fill up in the peak of July and August. Meanwhile, no pilgrim hostels exist on the Ruta do Mar (yet!), so walkers will need to stay in other accommodations. Of course, all pilgrims, regardless of route, are welcome to stay in any manner of accommodation. Some find the albergues to be a central part of the experience, while others need additional comfort at night in order to regroup for the next day's walk. Whenever possible, a range of options is presented for each stage in this guide, but other possibilities can always be found at

Rural lanes on the final stretch of the Inglés to Santiago (Inglés, Stage 5) (photo: Joe Williams)

the local tourist information office (turismo). Airbnb is increasingly an option worth exploring.

While the Spanish classification system for beds is not always on the mark, generally places identified as a *fonda* or *pensión* are designed for travelers on a budget. Furnishings and facilities are often a bit at the scruffier end of things. That said, they can be great deals. Those looking for more amenities will want to target *hostales* or *hoteles*, or in Galicia *hospedaxes*. The distinction between the two is not always clear, although hotels are typically stand-alone facilities with a receptionist available at all hours, while hostals fill only part of the building and provide guests with keys to their room, and the building, so they may come and go. The price is likely to be determined by the number of stars attributed to the facility.

FOOD

A pilgrim's culinary options are shaped in large part by the walking schedule and restaurant opening hours. In the morning, pilgrims can count on finding croissants and *cafés con leche*. Later in the day, those in need of something more substantial can ask for *bocadillos* – large sandwiches filled with a range of options, including ham (*jamón*), sausage (*chorizo*), cheese (*queso*), and omelette (*tortilla*). The *tortilla española* (egg and potato omelette) is a particularly filling snack on its own or in a bocadillo. Tapas – bite-sized appetizers, served both hot and cold – can be an excellent option for an evening snack.

A typical sitdown meal will involve a meat dish, a side dish, and bread. Vegetables are rarer, generally appearing in salads or soups. Fish is more abundant along the coast and throughout Galicia, so those who enjoy seafood will be living the good life on the Inglés and the Mar.

The greatest food-related challenge for many can be the Spanish meal schedule. Outside of cities, bars in the north rarely open before 0800, which is late for many pilgrims. Lunch, the major daily meal, is served between 1300 and 1500. Dinner presents the biggest difficulty, as it commonly begins around 2100, making it difficult to finish eating before the albergue curfew. Pilgrim-friendly bars and restaurants will serve earlier, but this varies greatly from town to town.

Some albergues have kitchens, where pilgrims can prepare their own meals. Groceries and supermarkets are accessible on most days, although some planning may be necessary, as they are not always located in the same towns as the albergues. Except in cities, they close during the siesta, so typical opening hours are from 0900 to 1300 and from 1600 to 2000. Almost every supermarket is closed on Sunday.

POSTAL SERVICES

Most post offices (*correos*) in Spain are open weekdays from 0830 until 1400. Some reopen in the afternoon and on Saturday mornings. Stamps can also be purchased from tobacco shops. The 'poste restante' system allows pilgrims (and everyone else) to send packages ahead, which comes in handy if you find yourself with unnecessary gear in your pack. While sending the gear home might be very expensive, mailing a package to Santiago is generally quite affordable. It is also an excellent way to receive care packages from home.

To mail a parcel poste restante, ask in the post office about Lista de Correos. If you do not have packing materials, most offices can provide these. On the mailing label, address the parcel to yourself, underlining your surname. Under your name, write 'Lista de Correos', followed by the postal code, town name, and province. Postal codes can be found on the www.correos.es website. Later, when you go to retrieve your package, make sure to take photo identification. The post office will generally hold packages for one month, but it is wise to reconfirm current policy when mailing.

TELEPHONES

Payphones are becoming an endangered species, but some still exist. Telephone cards can be purchased from tobacco shops; note that different cards are often needed for local and international calls. Instructions for making international calls are provided on each card. To call internationally, dial 00, wait for a new dial tone, and proceed with the country code, area code, and number. Spain's country code is 34; this can be dropped from numbers when you are calling within the country. Larger towns also have *locutorios* (call centers), which offer cheap international calls and internet connections. Most internet cafés have closed, likely as a consequence of the proliferation of smartphones; if you need an internet-connected terminal, your best bet is the local *biblioteca* (library), which often has a small computer lab. Bring your passport to check in.

More and more pilgrims are bringing their mobile phones with them on the camino. The most expensive way to do this is usually to activate an international package with your home provider, although this might make sense on a short pilgrimage like the Inglés. A more budget-friendly option is to purchase a pre-paid SIM card in Spain. Provided that your mobile phone is unlocked, you can put the Spanish SIM card in and immediately have a local number – and, by extension, local calling rates. Most companies, including Vodafone and MoviStar, have a very affordable starter pack available; credit can later be added online, by phone, and in many supermarkets. The cheapest approach, however, is to put your phone on airplane mode and use it exclusively as a WiFi device, making calls home through FaceTime or Skype and texting through WhatsApp, or similar programs.

OTHER LOCAL FACILITIES

Spanish banking hours are limited, typically running from around 0900 until 1400, Monday to Friday. Some banks open on Saturday morning. Almost every town has an ATM for withdrawing euros. Traveler's checks can be difficult to cash and are discouraged. Pharmacies are available in most towns and maintain a similar schedule to supermarkets. Medications, even basic items such as ibuprofen, are only available from pharmacies. Churches in most sizable towns hold mass on weekday and Saturday evenings, usually around 2000, as well as midday on Sundays. Ask in the albergue or listen for the bells. It is possible to ship your pack ahead on the Camino Inglés, but not the Mar. Your best bet is the service offered by the Spanish postal service, Correos, available April–October (www.elcaminoconcorreos.com). Expect to pay €4–5 per day.

WAYMARKING, ROUTE-PLANNING, AND MAPS

With occasional exceptions, the waymarking on the Camino Inglés is reliable. Trusty yellow arrows (*flechas amarillas*) painted on trees, signs, rocks, and other physical landmarks guide you through the countryside and most towns. Throughout Galicia, concrete markers complement the arrows, appearing regularly. With this reassurance, you should not have to clutch this book tightly each step of

Camino waymarking (photo: Joe Williams)

the way, nor should you count on it for turn-by-turn directions in all places. (The lone major exception is leaving A Coruña, where waymarks are supremely limited.)

By contrast, waymarking is highly inconsistent on the Ruta do Mar. The Camino Cantábrico sections are excellent and clear, while many portions of the local pilgrimage route to San Andrés de Teixido are quite good. The yellow arrows on the Mar specifically, however, are hit-or-miss. We encourage having access to gps tracks (available for download on the Cicerone site) while walking here, but if not some book-clutching is indeed appropriate.

Bear in mind that route changes are commonplace; indeed, significant portions of the Camino Inglés were re-routed in 2016–17. You may encounter waymarks that lead you in an unexpected direction. Study them carefully, evaluate your options, and make an informed choice. It is always wise to seek updated information from the hospitaleros.

The most useful single overview map of Galicia is the Michelin 'Spain: Northwest, Galicia' roadmap, which scales the region to 1:400,000. That's helpful for seeing the big picture, but not as useful for turn-by-turn navigation. The Spanish Mapas Militares (Serie L) are the best bet for more detailed route-finding assistance, designed on a 1:50,000 scale. The downside is that this is a much more expensive option, requiring you to

Shell waymarking on the Camino Inglés

purchase many individual map sheets to fully cover your route. The Mapas Militares are available from The Map Shop in the UK and can be ordered online.

GPX

GPX tracks for the routes in this guidebook are available to download free at www.cicerone.co.uk/1006/GPX. A GPS device is an excellent aid to navigation and recommended, but you should also carry a map and compass and know how to use them. GPX files are provided in good faith, but neither the author nor the publisher accept responsibility for their accuracy.

This guidebook has broken the Inglés and Mar into stages; each Inglés stage ends in a town or village with a pilgrim albergue, while all but one Mar stage ends in a town with accommodation options. Each stage of the Mar includes multiple route options, generally falling into two categories: a more direct 'Ruta do Mar' track and a coastal 'Camino Cantábrico' approach. We make specific suggestions on the preferred route for each stage, but provide short descriptions of both options. Bear in mind that these are simply recommendations and should in no way be considered the 'official' way of organizing the route. Listen to your body: if you're struggling, stop earlier; if you're flying,

Ferrol in the morning (Inglés, Stage 1)

enjoy it. Listen to your heart: if the beauty of a place strikes you, stick around. And listen to your fellow pilgrims: they may have excellent advice to offer.

The box at the start of each stage provides key information to help you assess the day ahead, including ratings of route-finding and terrain on a 1–5 scale. The figure for terrain indicates how physically demanding the stage is, with 1 corresponding to an easy walk and 5 to a very challenging trek. It is important to note that the difficulty rating does not factor in the day's distance. The route-finding rating indicates the challenge posed by the day's waymarking and presence of alternative routes. If you see a 1 or a 2, you can safely put away this book

and trust the waymarks. Anything higher suggests that there are some problematic stretches, or important route choices to make.

Key towns and villages along the route are shown in boxes in the route description (the distance from the previous key town/village is given after the heading). The boxes often include a short summary of features of interest, as well as information on accommodation and facilities.

With two languages spoken in Galicia – Castilian and Gallego – it can be challenging to achieve a single, consistent approach to place names. In this guidebook, names generally follow the Gallego spelling to reflect what is seen on street signs and maps. The similarity between Gallego and Castilian in most cases makes it easy to draw connections (for example, the words for church: 'Iglesia' and 'Igrexa').

This guide includes all pilgrim albergues in operation at the time of writing, and a range of selected hotels, hostels, and other viable options. All accommodation listings include price, phone numbers, and (when needed) address. Additional information includes the number of beds available, meals served, and the presence of cooking facilities, washer/dryer (W/D), and internet (@). Opening hours are also included if they are much later than normal, and where keys can be obtained if the albergue does not have an on-site hospitalero. Please note that prices, in particular, can change quickly or by season; always confirm in advance.

Each stage of the route in this guide is accompanied by a map at 1:100,000 scale. The maps use a red line for the main route description and a red dashed line for any alternative routes described. All place names in **bold** in the text are also included on the maps. Where a distance appears in brackets, that figure relates to the distance from the previous town/village that is highlighted in brackets.

N followed by a number (eg N-634) denotes a major Spanish highway, while regional roads are identified by the first two letters of the province followed by a number (eg AS-235).

The Appendices contain useful information sources on transport and other practicalities (Appendix A), a glossary of key terms in Spanish and Gallego (Appendix B), and some recommended further reading (Appendix C).

Finally, please bear in mind that the Ruta do Mar, in particular, is early in its redevelopment and there will be many, many changes to its arc in the years ahead. Our work to this point was inspired by fellow pilgrims who have been trailblazers, specifically Alan Sykes, 'Forestman,' Maggie Woodward (magwood.me), and T&V Brighton. Moving forward, we are grateful for all updates from readers and we are especially eager to hear from other pilgrims on their experiences on the Mar. Please get in touch: updates@cicerone.co.uk.

Covas shell house

CAMINO de SANTIAGO

CAMINO INGLÉS

THE CAMINO INGLÉS

The starting point of the Camino Inglés (photo: Joe Williams)

INTRODUCTION

For many pilgrims in earlier times, the beginning of the Camino Inglés would have marked the end of their pilgrimage's most dangerous section. This is where many seafaring pilgrims, especially from the British Isles and Scandinavia, would have made landfall and started their trek. Few, if any, of today's pilgrims will face such a journey. Instead, the biggest question is where to begin, as the Camino Inglés offers two different starting points. A Coruña is the more famous option, noted for its ancient lighthouse, the Tower of Hercules. However, the route from A Coruña to Santiago is less than 100km, making pilgrims who start there ineligible for the Compostela. As a result, many pilgrims start in Ferrol, another major port town, from where the route is long enough to earn a Compostela. The two branches of the Inglés unite in Hospital de Bruma (at the end of Stage 3), 41km from Santiago. Those seeking peaceful Galician countryside and little pilgrim traffic will find both here. Despite its proximity to Santiago and its excellent waymarking, the route remains lightly used, especially outside of summer.

Church near Ferrol (Stage 1)

STAGE 1
Ferrol to Pontedeume

Start	Curuxeiras dock, Ferrol
Finish	Albergue de Peregrinos, Pontedeume
Distance	29.5km
% unpaved	27.9%
Total ascent	457m
Total descent	457m
Terrain	2
Route-finding	3
Pilgrim accommodation	Neda, Pontedeume

The Camino Inglés begins at the ocean's edge at the port of Ferrol. Begin your walk at the dock of Curuxeiras and continue through the town center before returning back toward the water. Enjoy the beach and sea views before heading inland, when the walk leads through the industrial and suburban outskirts of Ferrol on the way to Neda. After a short stint through gentle hills, the end of today's walk returns to the coast once again; the beach is just off-route as you skirt the edge of Cabañas and follow the long bridge into Pontedeume, where the albergue enjoys a waterfront location. While the waymarking is generally reliable, urban walking can always be a little tricky (cars like to park in front of waymarks!), so pay close attention.

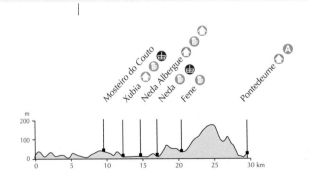

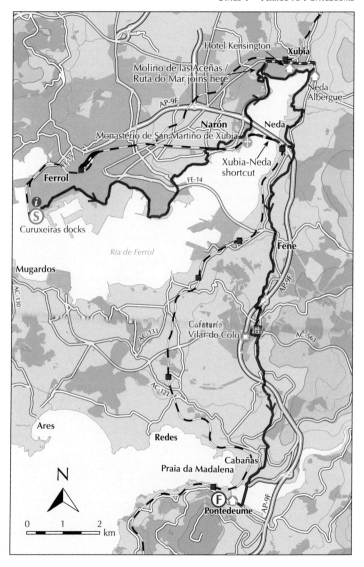

FERROL

All facilities. RENFE/FEVE station. **Hostal La Frontera** (singles €22–26, doubles €30–34, meals available, @, c/San Andres 4, tel 881 953 036), **Hostal Porta Nova II** (singles €18, doubles €30, c/Naturalista López Seone 33–35, tel 981 359 772), **Hotel Silva** (singles €27–32, doubles €36–44, triples €43–51, quads €50–58, open all year, @, Río Castro, tel 981 310 552), **Hotel El Suizo** (singles €49–55, doubles €56–62, breakfast available, @, c/Rúa Dolores, tel 981 300 400). The main tourist office is located near the train station in the Praza de España, making it an easy visit after arrival (open daily in summer 1000–1300, 1700–1900, reduced hours in off-season, tel 981 944 251). A second turismo, oriented toward pilgrims, is located next to the Inglés' starting point in the port (open daily in summer 0900–1300, 1500–1930; in off-season, open Mon–Fri 0930–1230, Sat–Sun 1000–1300, 1600–1800; tel 981 944 252). Credenciales are available from both turismos, as well as the concatedral (€2).

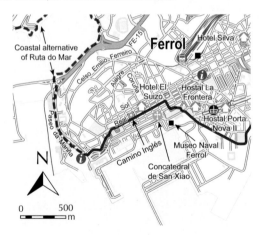

Ferrol has long been an important port city, given its strategic military position, naval academy, and its major shipbuilding facilities. It was also the launch-point for the (ultimately unsuccessful) Spanish Armada in 1588. General Francisco Franco was born here, and from 1938 to 1982 the name of the city was officially changed to 'El Ferrol del Caudillo'. Its seafaring history is evocatively presented in the **Museo Naval Ferrol** (open Mon–Fri 0930–1330, Sat–Sun 1030–1330), located in former prison barracks in the port. Its model ships, including a stunning one of the *Santa María Magdalena*, are worth the visit. The **Concatedral de San Xiao** shares the episcopal see with Mondoñedo's cathedral on the Camino del Norte. A relatively recent construction, dating to the 18th century (and built on the remains of an earlier Romanesque temple), the concatedral unusually adheres to a Greek cross layout, instead of the Latin norm. Castle-lovers with time on their hands should make the 15-minute drive out to **Castelo de San Felipe** (1000–1400, 1600–2000), situated on the coast to the west of Ferrol.

The Camino Inglés begins from Ferrol's central port. ▶ The first stone waymark is just before the arch leading to c/Carmen Curuxeiras. The route through Ferrol is well marked, leading from the port past the Igrexa de San Francisco and then along Rúa Real to the Praza de Armas. Wrap through Praza da Constitución, Praza das Angustias, and leave the old town on Rúa Taxonera (quickly becoming Avda Macmahon). Following a windy stroll through Ferrol's sprawl, arrive at the coastline 3.5km from the port; this becomes your close companion for much of the walk to Neda's albergue.

To earn the Compostela, it is essential that you obtain your first stamp before leaving Ferrol: this could be from the concatedral, the turismo, your accommodation, or a bar.

The next 6km generally proceeds along wide sidewalks and coastal promenades, with periodic opportunities to drop down closer to the waterfront. Pass the waterfront Ermida de Santa María de Caranza and its neighboring Praia de Caranza, then cut under the expressway. A large shopping complex is on the other side, with two major supermarkets. A very brief inland jaunt follows, navigating around train tracks and passing through O Vila de Fiasca, with waymarks leading straight through the neighborhood and then downhill to the 12th-century church of **Monasterio de San Martiño de Xubia** (Mosteiro do Couto), formerly part of a larger Benedictine monastic complex.

Shortcut

Those seeking a shorter day can pursue a shortcut here, turning right and crossing the pedestrian bridge over the Ría de Ferrol. Just before the **Neda station**, turn left and

Monasterio de San Martiño de Xubia (photo: Joe Williams)

then right immediately after, passing under A-8. Cross N-642, turn right, and then left immediately after, rejoining the official route. This trims 6.4km off the day's walk.

Continue straight past the church, forking right soon after to return to the riverside track. After a pleasant coastal stretch, the route runs alongside FE-11, before wrapping back under it and arriving at the old mill (Molino de las Aceñas) on the riverside, 2.6km from the church. Yet another shortcut is possible here, continuing straight over the river alongside FE-11 and rejoining the Inglés on the other side. Cross a small stone dam, proceed 500 meters along the river, and then face another decision. ◄ If you'd like to access the shops, bars, and accommodation in neighboring Narón and Xubia (**Hotel Kensington** – singles €21, doubles €29, meals available, sello, Crta de Castilla 832, tel 981 387 326; **Hotel Marcial** – singles €22, doubles €33, meals available, c/Río Pereiro 6-8, tel 981 384 417), turn left and then right immediately after. Follow this until you cross a bridge; turn right on the other side and join a riverside pedestrian track. Alternatively, turn right and remain on the coastal promenade (**fountains**). After crossing a pedestrian bridge, rejoin the other route and arrive at the

The 'Ruta do Mar' intersects from the left immediately after the dam, waymarked for the local pilgrimage to San Andrés de Teixido – see Mar, Stage 7.

NEDA ALBERGUE (14.5KM)

Albergue de Peregrinos (€6, 28 beds, open all year, kitchen, tel 629 224 622/981 390 233). **Pensión Maragoto** is just north, on the highway (singles €15–27, doubles €29–40, Avda do Xubia 12, tel 981 347 304).

Following 1km more on the promenade, veer inland, wrapping around the Iglesia de Santa María (sello from adjacent parish building) and a playground. Join c/ Paraíso, which becomes Rúa Real, and proceed into

NEDA (2.1KM)

Bars, grocery, pharmacy. Internet and sello in **Casa da Cultura**, on the main road.

The Gothic **Igrexa de San Nicolás** dates to the 14th century, but was subsequently refurbished in the baroque style. It is a site of local pilgrimages on Mondays (known as 'St Nicholas Walks'), for those seeking intervention from the so-called 'lawyer of difficult cases.'

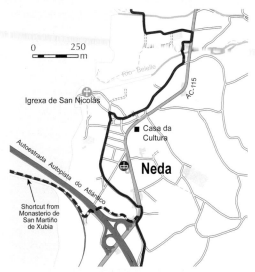

Neda's Albergue de Peregrinos

Leaving Neda, the route also leaves the coast, climbing into the modest hills. Quiet, minor roads proceed roughly parallel to AC-115, crossing the expressway and then delivering you into **Fene** (bars) 3.7km later. Two pilgrim-friendly bars offer meals and sellos at the highway crossing, and the Casa do Concello soon after offers a sello as well.

The walk continues roughly parallel to N-651, following minor roads southward through Perlio and Mundín. Just 1.1km later, fork onto a footpath, passing under the Viaduct Romariz. Emerge on the edge of an industrial center 2km later, with **Cafetería Vilar do Colo** on your right at a roundabout. Turn left at the roundabout, then right onto N-651, briefly joining the highway before forking left uphill. After a second stint on N-651, the camino veers right shortly after Bar Victor onto a path. Cross the expressway and then begin the day's final descent, enjoying excellent views of Pontedeume unfolding beneath you. The route skirts the edge of **Cabañas** (bar), a pleasant beach town, joining N-651 once more to cross the Río Eume. Turn right immediately after the bridge and proceed 200 meters to the albergue in

PONTEDEUME (12.9KM)

All facilities. **Albergue de Peregrinos** (€6, 20 beds, open all year, W/D, @, Avda de Marina, tel 981 433 039), **Hostal Allegue** (doubles €30–40, c/Chafarís 1, tel 981 430 035), **Hostal Luís** (doubles €25–42, c/San Augustín 12, tel 981 430 235), **Hotel Eumesa** (€70–80, includes breakfast, Avda da Coruña, tel 981 430 925).

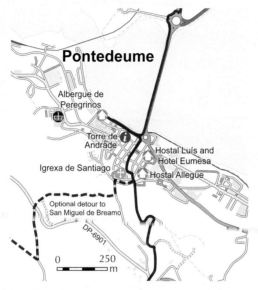

A picturesque town situated between hills and the Río Eume. The powerful Andrade family originated in Pontedeume in the Middle Ages, influenced the town's development, and commissioned many of the city's (and region's) architectural gems. Its 18th-century **Igrexa de Santiago** includes the tomb of Fernando de Andrade, an acclaimed military figure from the 16th century.

The **Pontedeume Bridge**, with 14th-century origins but a current structure dating to the 19th century, was commissioned by Fernán Pérez de Andrade, the family patriarch. It originally had 116 arches and a chapel located between arches 21 and 22. The **Torreón dos Andrade**, located in the town center, is all that remains of the grand 14th-century Pazo dos Condes. Currently the tower houses Pontedeume's tourist office and the Andrade Interpretation Center. The 12th-century **Igrexa de San Miguel de Breamo** is an impressive

43

early Romanesque church situated 3km outside of town; legends suggest that it was built over a Celtic temple's remains. Another story claims that its rose window's 11 tips harken back to the 11 Knights Templar who guarded it.

Pontedeume and its impressive bridge

STAGE 2

Pontedeume to Betanzos

Start	Albergue de Peregrinos, Pontedeume
Finish	Albergue de Peregrinos, Betanzos
Distance	20.7km
% unpaved	26.7%
Total ascent	563m
Total descent	537m
Terrain	4
Route-finding	1
Pilgrim accommodation	Miño, Betanzos

Bid farewell to the coast's beaches and ports, instead turning inland toward green hills and peaceful villages. Prepare for a steep climb out of Pontedeume, for which you will be rewarded with great views of the city below. Those who have time could consider detouring to the early Romanesque church of San Miguel de Breamo, nestled on the hillside above Pontedeume. The route continues through the countryside, offering one significant rest stop for food and supplies in Miño, before eventually leading to the medieval town of Betanzos. Betanzos is a major highlight of the Inglés, with lively plazas, shady parks, and a lovely historic core.

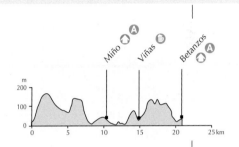

Coastal alternative

A coastal alternative is possible between Pontedeume and Miño. It's unmarked, but includes a lengthy section of footpath, two extended beaches, and some minor high-way walking (mostly with sidewalks). To join it, walk to Pontedeume's train station, cross the tracks, and find the footpath at the far side of the platform. This approach is 2.8km longer than the official route, but often quite lovely.

Backtrack from the albergue and proceed uphill through town on c/Real. Turn left just before the Igrexa de Santiago, then right onto c/San Augustín. ▶ Proceed uphill, making a series of well-marked turns as you leave town. Some 2.6km from the albergue the ascent concludes; turn left downhill, passing a picnic area. The next 2.4km is mostly off-road, with quite varied scenery, including an arbor, woods, a short highway stint, and a golf course. Turn left and cross AP-9/E-1.

To visit San Miguel de Breamo, instead pass behind the church and follow Rúa Fontenova south, before turning right on a footpath soon after.

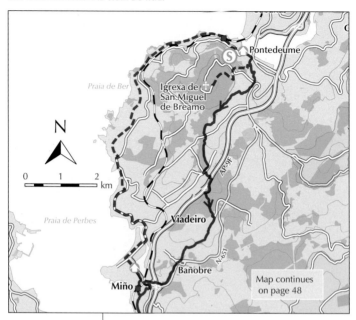

Miño's stunning beach is worth a short detour from the town center

The next 3km lead through the villages of **Viadeiro** and **Bañobre**. Cross the Baxoi Bridge and turn right onto a footpath along the river, passing under the bridge and the expressway (several times). Turn right onto a minor road, then onto the Rúa Fonte, leading into

MIÑO (10.1KM)

Bars, grocery, pharmacy. **Albergue de Peregrinos** (€6, 22 beds, open all year, kitchen, Rúa Marismas, tel 607 803 569). **Pensión O Cantiño** (singles €25, doubles €38, c/Loyos 39, tel 981 782 007). **Hostal La Terraza** (singles €30–35, doubles €48–55, triples/quads, includes breakfast, tel 657 629 292).

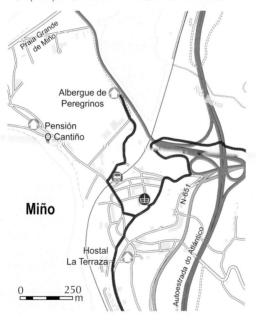

To reach the albergue, fork right (waymarked) and proceed 750 meters to the outskirts of town. Otherwise, fork left to continue. At the end of town, fork right

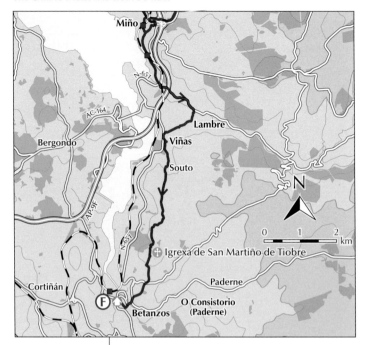

downhill. Cross the railroad and turn right along the coast. Turn right after **Mesón Almeda** and pass under N-651. Turn left and then right immediately after, joining a riverside road. Some 3.1km from Miño, turn right and cross a stone bridge. Follow minor roads into **Lambre** and then back to N-651 in **Viñas (bar)**, 1.5km later.

Fork left off the highway and follow a series of minor roads through the hills, leading 2.8km to **Souto** and then another kilometer to the **Igrexa de San Martiño de Tiobre**. Wind through lightly-populated hills and past the Santuario de Nosa Señora do Camiño before rejoining N-651, 1.6km later, for the final approach to Betanzos. Cross the Río Mandeo, pass through the arch, and turn left uphill. Turn right in the Praza de Constitución and proceed 200 meters to the albergue in

BETANZOS (10.6KM)

All facilities. **Albergue de Peregrinos Casa de Pescadería** (€6, 35 beds, open all year, tel 981 687 001), **Pensión Betanzos Chocolateria** (singles €15, doubles €30, c/Pintor Seijo Rubio 1, tel 981 774 495), **Pensión Cheiño** (singles €15, doubles €30, Rúa Venezuela 35, tel 981 773 128), **Hotel Garelos** (singles €37–55, doubles €50–75, includes breakfast, c/Alfonso IX 8, tel 981 775 922), **Pensión El Hórreo** (singles €15, doubles €30, Rúa Venezuela 26–28, tel 669 191 387). Turismo en route, just after Praza dos Irmáns García Naveira (Mon–Fri 1000–1400, 1600–1900, Sat 1030–1300, tel 981 776 666).

Betanzos originated as a Galician port town in the 13th century, but the port subsequently silted up. It has since become a bustling market town. The 14th-century **Iglesia de San Francisco** was commissioned by Fernán Pérez de Andrade and contains his tomb. The 15th-century **Iglesia de Santiago** features a Santiago Matamoros above the main portal. Attached to the church is a 16th-century clocktower. Much of Betanzos is still surrounded by its medieval wall. The **Parque del Pasatiempo** (1000–1300 and 1600–2030) is a unique spot, preserving an ambitious sculpture garden that, while vastly reduced from its origins a century ago, is well worth a visit.

The historic town of Betanzos

Fountain on the approach to Betanzos (photo: Joe Williams)

STAGE 3
Betanzos to Hospital de Bruma

Start	Albergue de Peregrinos, Betanzos
Finish	Albergue de Peregrinos, Hospital de Bruma
Distance	25.7km
% unpaved	39.6%
Total ascent	749m
Total descent	384m
Terrain	3
Route-finding	1
Pilgrim accommodation	Presedo, Hospital de Bruma

Today's walk brings you into the heart of rural Galicia. Plan to enjoy breakfast in Betanzos – the only sizable town on the itinerary – before climbing out, and be sure to pack some supplies. You won't see another grocery store until Sigüeiro. Presedo offers today's lone rest stop with food. Otherwise, it's all small farms and wooded countryside, with village churches in Cos and Leiro to break the walk. Recent route changes have eliminated the most strenuous ascent on the Inglés; instead, after Presedo the stage pushes harder to the west, past a pleasant park at the Beche reservoir (*embalse*). There's still plenty of uphill, but it's more gradual, leading into Hospital de

Bruma – a historically important pilgrim stop on the Camino Inglés, where the routes from Ferrol and A Coruña converge. The albergue is fantastic, although facilities in town are limited.

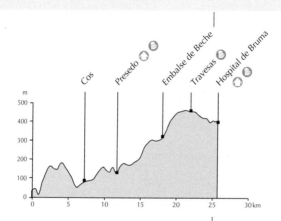

Backtrack to the Praza de Constitución and cross southward, toward the Iglesia de Santo Domingo. Keep the church on your left and continue onto Rúa do Rollo. After descending to cross a bridge, turn left and begin climbing up minor roads. Cross the railroad and A-6, then turn right downhill. Pass through **Liminón**, 3.9km from Betanzos, and transition onto a dirt track. Turn right onto a minor road, cross the river and bear left toward **Cos**, 3.6km from Liminón.

The next stretch involves many turns in quick succession, leading 1.8km past the Igrexa de Santiago de Meangos. Continue on a series of minor roads and dirt tracks running generally parallel to DP-0105, before joining it and then forking left onto a dirt road into

PRESEDO (12.3KM)

Albergue de Peregrinos (€6, 16 beds, open all year, kitchen, tel 606 274 430).

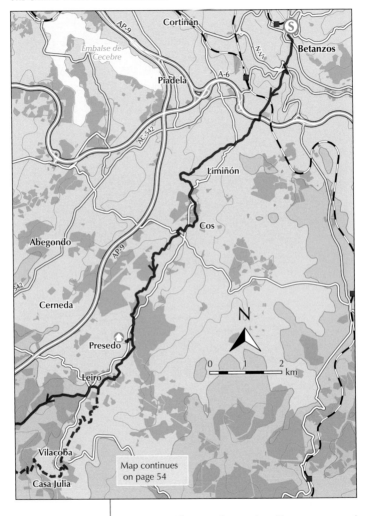

Map continues
on page 54

Keep straight on, as the paved road becomes unpaved
once again, leading 600 meters to the excellent Meson-
Museo Xente No Camino (bar). Follow a series of winding

The church of Leiro

roads 1.5km to the church of **Leiro**. A recent route change calls for a right turn at the T-junction after the church. Join a dirt track through the trees for the next 3km (rest area with toilets by **Embalse de Beche**). ▶ Turn left, and then fork right under the expressway. After passing through a small village, rejoin a forest track 900 meters later. Continue for 3.1km to meet a minor road. Turn right and left onto a slightly larger road in **As Travesas**. The route starting from A Coruña intersects from the right.

After 1.4km, turn left onto a dirt road, later turning right onto another dirt track. Transition onto a paved road just before arriving in

The old route, still on the map, involves more pavement and a significant ascent, but also offers a bar, Casa Julia.

HOSPITAL DE BRUMA (13.4KM)

Bar/restaurant. **Albergue de Peregrinos** (€6, 22 beds, open all year, kitchen, tel 981 692 921).

Hospital de Bruma is significant for its position as the junction between the two Inglés routes. The current albergue is located in a restored medieval pilgrim hospital. Pilgrims interested in walking the A Coruña leg of the Inglés can catch a bus from neighboring **Mesón do Vento** (**Pensión Mesón Novo** – singles €26–37, doubles €42–46, tel 981 692 776), 1.5km away, and those desperate for snacks may find its gas station shop handy. The hospitalero at Bruma has updated bus schedules available.

The charming albergue of Hospital de Bruma

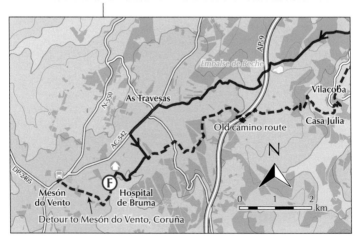

STAGE 4
Hospital de Bruma to Sigüeiro

Start	Albergue de Peregrinos, Hospital de Bruma
Finish	Albergue Miras, Sigüeiro
Distance	24.7km
% unpaved	30.9%
Total ascent	273m
Total descent	437m
Terrain	1
Route-finding	1
Pilgrim accommodation	Sigüeiro

This stage divides tidily into two halves. The first proceeds mostly due south along paved roads through a series of eight small villages. Buscás provides an ideal stopping point for breakfast, while Calle de Poulo is your last chance at supplies until the walk's end. After that, the Camino bends to a more southwestwardly trajectory, spending much more time off-pavement and in uninhabited countryside. The final stretch parallels the expressway, wrapping around an industrial plant, before finally entering Sigüeiro through a pleasant, shady park. After two days of very limited facilities, Sigüeiro – a small town – may feel like a booming metropolis!

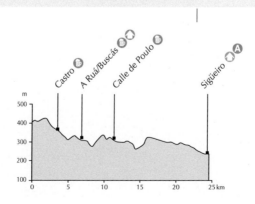

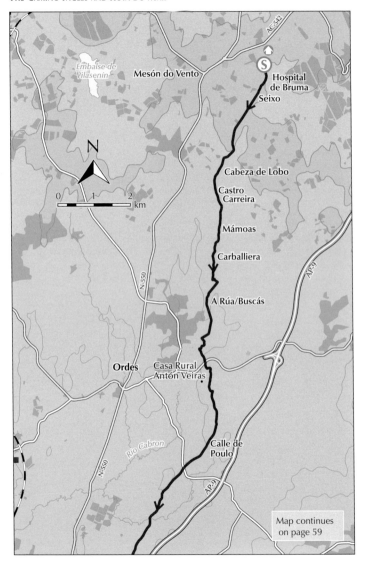

Embalse de Vilasenín

Mesón do Vento

S Hospital de Bruma

Seixo

N

0 1 2 km

Cabeza de Lobo

Castro Carreira

Mámoas

Carballiera

A Rúa/Buscás

N-550

AP-9

Ordes

Casa Rural Antón Veiras

Río Cabrón

Calle de Poulo

N-550

AP-9

Map continues on page 59

Keep straight on through a series of villages: **Seixo**, **Cabeza de Lobo** (bar), **Carreira**, **Mámoas**, and **Carballiera**. Fork right onto a dirt track; later, turn right onto a minor road into

A RÚA/BUSCÁS (7KM)

Bars. **Bar Novo** serves food. **Casa Rural Dona María** (doubles, prices vary by season, meals available, tel 981 680 040).

The Romanesque **Igrexa de San Paio de Buscás** was restored in the 19th century.

Proceed 2.1km along minor roads, passing under AC-524. Curve left, skirting **Casa Rural Antón Veiras** (doubles €50–60, triple €75, @, meals available, tel 981 682 303). Follow a footpath and then rural roads 2.6km to **Calle de Poulo**, which is the last town with provisions before Sigüeiro.

Cross under AC-3802 and join a small paved road. Follow another well-marked mix of dirt and paved roads for 6km, then cross under AP-9. Turn right on the other side; the next 4.5km proceed roughly alongside the expressway, following dirt tracks. Just before an industrial plant, fork left and then turn right 400 meters later.

The church of Buscás

Follow this 1.2km and then turn left onto a footpath. Pass to the right of the swimming pool and then proceed directly toward the Concello de Oroso. Turn left and then take the next right on Rúa Río Lengüelle. Turn left on Rúa do Tambre and then right on Rúa Camiño Real. Turn left on the main road, in the center of

SIGÜEIRO (17.7KM)

All facilities. **Albergue O Fogar da Chisca** (€16, 12 beds, includes breakfast, kitchen, W/D, @, Rúa do Campo 4, tel 638 177 894), **Albergue Camiño Real** (€15, 23 beds, doubles €40–50, open all year, W/D, tel 685 110 377), **Albergue Miras** (€13, 14 beds, open all year, includes laundry, kitchen, Avda de Compostela 16, tel 881 981 909). **Sigüeiro Hostel** (singles €26–36, doubles €40–60, Plaza Alexandre Bóveda 1, tel 981 973 636).

The 14th-century **Romanesque bridge** was built by Fernán Pérez de Andrade, although there is some speculation that he only rebuilt a 13th-century structure.

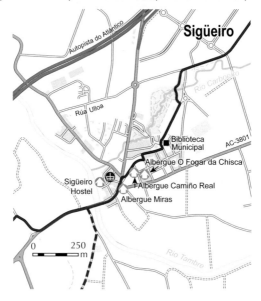

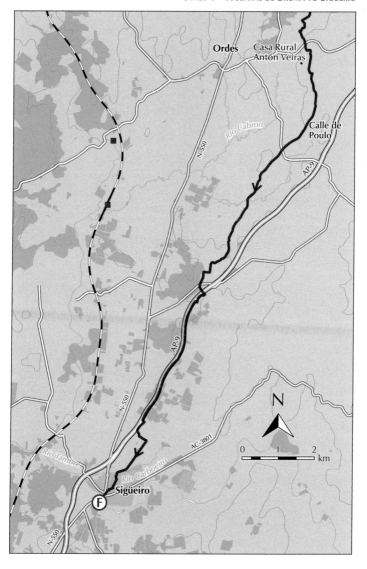

STAGE 5

Sigüeiro to Santiago de Compostela

Start	Albergue Miras, Sigüeiro
Finish	Praza do Obradoiro, Santiago de Compostela
Distance	16.2km
% unpaved	37.7%
Total ascent	264m
Total descent	238m
Terrain	2
Route-finding	2
Pilgrim accommodation	Santiago de Compostela

Get ready for Santiago! This is a short stage, making it possible for you to arrive in Santiago in time for the noon pilgrim mass, if you get off to an early start. There are few opportunities en route for food prior to Santiago's outskirts, so plan accordingly. The walk as a whole is fairly unremarkable, running generally parallel to N-550 and involving few ascents or descents of note. But at day's end, you'll be in Santiago, your pilgrimage complete and the baroque cathedral spires towering overhead!

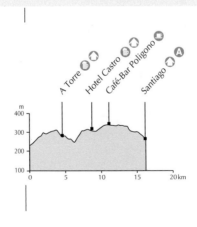

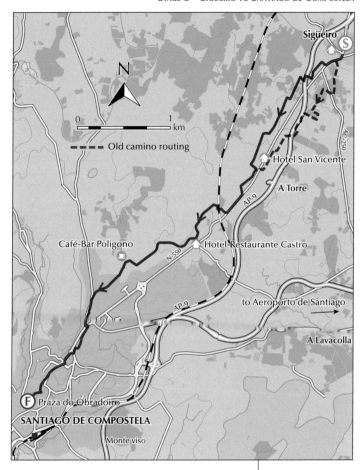

- - - - Old camino routing

Proceed through Sigüeiro, cross the Río Tambre and continue along N-550 for 600 meters. ▶ Turn right and then left, and then right again, following a minor road across E-8. Turn left on the other side and then continue to zigzag through quiet countryside, following minor roads and dirt tracks to the edge of

The old route, forking left off of the highway outside of Sigüeiro, is still preferred by some and included on the map.

A TORRE (4.7KM)

Bar. **Hotel San Vicente** (doubles €67, c/Marantes 12, tel 981 694 571), located on N-550.

Continue along N-550. Fork right onto a minor road, cross the railroad, and then turn left onto a dirt track. Proceed through the woods and then loop behind **Hotel-Restaurante Castro** (singles €41, doubles €50, tel 981 509 304), 3.8km from A Torre. Continue 2.5km through the 'Bosque Encantado' (Enchanted Forest) and then alongside an industrial plant, before turning left to enter it with **Café-Bar Poligono** on right.

Keep straight on for 1.7km, ultimately joining Rúa do Tambre. Shortly after Bar Miro, fork left, following Rúa do Meixonfrío before rejoining Tambre. Descend to N-634, cross it using the crosswalk to your left, and then proceed straight ahead, curving to the right, on Rúa de Mallou. Continue straight through a minor intersection, then fork right. Shortly after it curves right, turn left and proceed to a major intersection. Pass to the left of a McDonald's, cross N-634, and then turn right on the other side,

Santiago Cathedral

following a pedestrian walkway as it curves left. Perform a similar maneuver at the next roundabout, continuing straight on Rúa da Pastoriza, which becomes Rúa dos Basquiños, Rúa de Santa Clara, and Rúa de San Roque in quick succession. Fork right onto Rúa Santa Clara as you pass the Convento de Santa Clara.

You are now entering the old town of Santiago – only 800 meters remain! Follow the road as it winds through compact quarters, becoming Rúa dos Loureiros, Rúa da Porta da Pena, Rúa da Fonte de San Miguel, and then Rúa da Troia. Turn right to proceed into the Praza da Inmaculada, descend steps through the arch, and arrive in the Praza do Obradoiro in

SANTIAGO DE COMPOSTELA (11.5KM)

Congratulations! Upon arrival in Santiago, you have two main pilgrim destinations remaining. First and foremost is the cathedral (open 0700–2000 daily). Access to a statue of the apostle Saint James (for hugging purposes) is limited to 0930–1320 and 1600–1900 daily. Pilgrims may visit the apostle's relics all day. Confessions (possible in multiple languages) are heard 0800–1300 and 1700–2100 daily. Pilgrim mass takes place from 1200–1300 and 1930–2030 daily; arrive early. Second is the Pilgrim's Office (Rúa Carretas 33), which issues Compostelas (0800–2000, shorter winter hours). You are not required to pick this up on the day of arrival; pilgrims continuing to Finisterre may prefer to obtain their Compostela upon return.

Santiago has a wide range of accommodation. Albergue options include: **San Lázaro** (€10, 80 beds, kitchen, W/D, Rúa San Lázaro, tel 981 571 488), **Seminario Menor** (€10–15, 199 beds, W/D, Rúa de Belvís, tel 881 031 768), **The Last Stamp** (€15, 62 beds, kitchen, W/D, @, Rúa do Preguntoiro 10, tel 981 563 525), **Porta Real** (€10–20, 24 beds, W/D, @, c/Concheiros 10, tel 633 610 114), **Mundoalbergue** (€16–18, 34 beds, kitchen, W/D, c/San Clemente 26, tel 981 588 625), and **Roots & Boots** (€16–20, kitchen, W/D, c/del Campo del Crucero del Gallo 7, tel 699 631 594). In most cases, reservations are accepted and pilgrims can stay multiple nights. Other options include: **Hostal Suso** (doubles €40–49, Rúa do Vilar 65, tel 981 586 611), **Hostal Costa Azul** (singles €30, doubles €37+, Rúa das Galeras 18, tel 602 451 906), **Hostal Alfonso** (singles €35–50, doubles €45–70, Rúa do Pombal 40, tel 981 585 685), and **Hospedería San Martín Pinario** (singles €50+, doubles €57+, Plaza Inmaculada 3, tel 981

560 282). For a splurge, consider Santiago's Parador, the **Hostal de los Reyes Católicos** (doubles €155+, Praza do Obradoiro, tel 981 582 200). Once upon a time, this was a pilgrim hospital, founded by Ferdinand and Isabel.

Buses to Labacolla airport run daily every 30min between 0610 and 0010. The trip takes 25min. The central bus station is located roughly 2km from the cathedral in Praza Camilo Díaz Baliño. The RENFE station is a similar distance in the opposite direction. Those hoping to visit Finisterre as a daytrip may find it more convenient to arrange this through their albergue, as minibus tours lessen the drive time significantly and offer a competitive price. Head south of the cathedral for Santiago's most lively areas. Rúa do Franco, Rúa do Vilar, and Rúa Nova offer popular restaurants, bars packed full of celebrating pilgrims, souvenir shops, and bookstores. The Correos is just off Franco on Travesa de Fonseca. If city life is too much after so many peaceful days, keep straight on along Franco, cross out of the old town, and proceed into the Alameda, a large, green park with many quiet corners.

Although there is much to see and do in Santiago, many pilgrims are drawn back to the Praza do Obradoiro many times, reliving the moment of arrival as new waves of pilgrims surge in front of the cathedral and reunite with friends from the walk. For those having walked the Camino Inglés, it can be more than a little overwhelming, encountering so many new pilgrims. But it is a powerful reminder of the larger community to which you all now belong, pilgrims on the Camino de Santiago, owners of the Compostela.

The altar of Santiago Cathedral

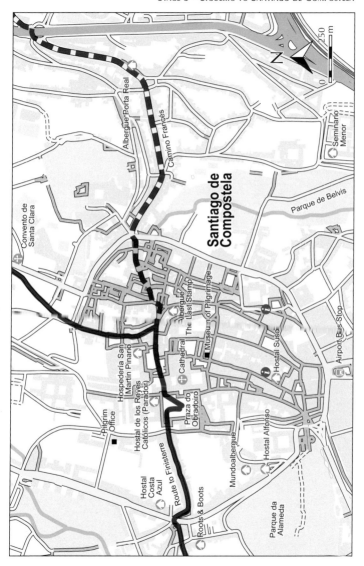

Santiago de Compostela

Albergue Porta Real

Camino Francés

Seminario Menor

Parque de Belvis

Convento de Santa Clara

The Last Stamp

Albergue

Museum of Pilgrimage

Hospedería San Martín Pinario

Cathedral

Hostal Suso

Pilgrim Office

Hostal de los Reyes Católicos (Parador)

Praza do Obradoiro

Airport Bus-Stop

Hostal Alfonso

Mundoalbergue

Hostal Costa Azul

Route to Finisterre

Roots & Boots

Parque da Alameda

ALTERNATIVE START
A Coruña to Hospital de Bruma

Start	Igrexa de Santiago, A Coruña
Finish	Albergue de Peregrinos, Hospital de Bruma
Distance	33.6km
% unpaved	18.5%
Total ascent	902m
Total descent	528m
Terrain	3
Route-finding	4
Pilgrim accommodation	Sergude-Carral, Hospital de Bruma

A Coruña was historically the favored starting point for pilgrims walking to Santiago. The busy port city is only 75km from Santiago; while this made A Coruña a popular starting point in the Middle Ages, it is a deterrent for pilgrims today, who must walk at least 100km to Santiago in order to receive the Compostela. The route begins from the Igrexa de Santiago, located in the historic center of A Coruña, and traditionally the first stopping point on the pilgrimage. The visit to A Coruña may be the highlight of today's route; after leaving the old town, the camino passes through industrial areas and suburbs for most of the walk. That said, there are some wonderfully enjoyable stretches as well, including a waterfront jaunt to O Burgo and a peaceful country stroll past Sigrás.

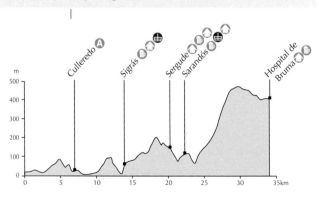

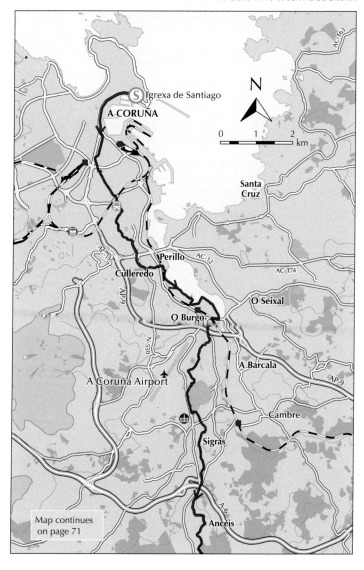

A CORUÑA

All facilities. RENFE station. Airport 8km from the city, offering domestic and international connections. **Pensión Residencia Nogallas** (singles €25–30, doubles €35–50, c/Julio Rodriguez Yordi 11, tel 981 262 100), **Pensión Las Rias** (singles €25+, doubles €30+, San Andres 141, tel 981 226 879), **Hotel Santa Catalina** (singles €30, doubles €44, Fernando Arenas Quintela 1, tel 981 226 704).

A prosperous and strategically located port city, A Coruña has been important since Romans established it as a trade center in the first and second centuries. Traces of Roman rule can be found in the **Tower of Hercules** (€3, open 1000–2100 Jun–Sep, 1000–1800 Oct–May), built during Trajan's reign. Located on the edge of the peninsula, it is the oldest functioning lighthouse in the world.

In 1589, Sir Francis Drake embarked on a mission to sack A Coruña. A 13-day battle ensued, during which María Pita's husband was killed. When she heard this news, she took to arms in his stead and killed one of the English soldiers scaling the city walls, inspiring the women of A Coruña to join the battle and seize victory. The **Praza de María Pita** is named after her and features a dramatic 20th-century neoclassical Municipal Palace.

The grand Praza de María Pita

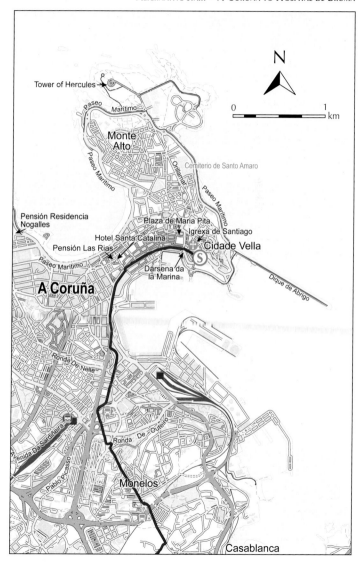

The 12th-century Romanesque **Igrexa de Santiago** (Mon–Fri 1100–1330 and 1830–1930) is the oldest church in A Coruña. It has been renovated over the centuries and now features Gothic arches, a baroque altarpiece, and two 18th-century rose windows. A Coruña is sometimes called the 'Crystal City' because the **Dársena de la Marina**, glass-enclosed galleries on the seaside promenade, reflect sunlight back toward the sea.

Waymarks are almost non-existent in the city center.

◀ From the Igrexa de Santiago's west door, descend Rúa de Santiago and continue straight along Avda Montoto (becoming Avda de Marina). Alternatively, it is possible to turn right into the Praza de María Pita, with the turismo to the right. Pass an obelisk and join c/Cantón Grande, crossing to the other side of the street and continuing forward. Keep straight on as the road becomes Avda de Linares Rivas. Ascend the overpass to Avda de Alcalde Alfonso Molina. Fork left on Avda Latorre, cross a complicated intersection (with a large fountain on your left), and then fork right on c/Marqués de Amboage. As this road curves left, it becomes Rúa de Caballeros and passes the bus station, 2.6km from the center.

Pass under the highway and navigate through a busy roundabout, with the goal being to continue straight on Avda dos Monelos. Then, at another complicated roundabout, with three possible forks, take the upper-left option past an Eroski supermarket, which continues to be Avda dos Monelos. Turn right onto a minor road; at this point, waymarks become more common and reliable. Make your way through suburbs, then turn right onto the highway. Cross the expressway – take care here! – and continue downhill, passing a giant Alcampo store on your right. Roughly 1km after that, watch attentively for a left turn, which leads downhill into

CULLEREDO (6.8KM)

All facilities. **Hotel Crunia** (singles €45, doubles €50, meals available, @, Avda Fonteculler 58, tel 981 650 088), **Hotel a Barquiña** (singles €33, doubles €55, includes breakfast, @, Plaza de Santa Gema 7, tel 981 662 402).

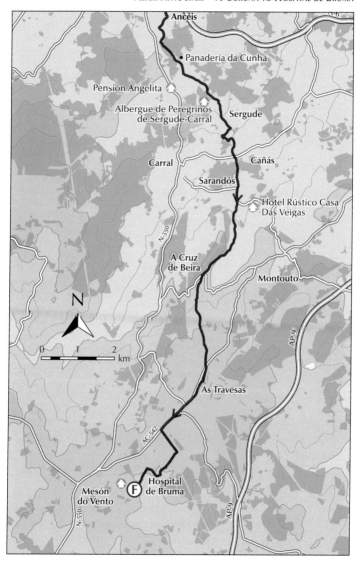

Turn right onto a promenade, enjoying a long stretch on the Ría do Burgo. Waymarks dry up again in this stretch, but just stay on the waterfront. When you arrive at a bridge, turn right uphill in

O BURGO (2.9KM)

All facilities. **Hostal O Mesón** (Avda da Coruña 25, tel 981 660 065).

The **Bridge of Burgo** was the specific target of Sir John Moore's last mission during the Peninsular Wars. After being ravaged by dynamite, it remained in a state of disrepair until the late 20th century. The Romanesque **Igrexa de Santiago do Burgo** was given to the archbishop of Santiago in the 12th century (sello). On the bridge's east side stands the **Igrexa de Santa María do Temple**; as its name suggests, its founding is linked with the Knights Templar, as is the original bridge.

Cross a railroad and turn left, following a minor road as it curves to the right. Turn left on Avda de Galicia and pass under the expressway. Fork right onto Rúa Pelamios and continue uphill, passing the Igrexa de San Xiao de Almeiras, then descend to a road running alongside N-550, 3km from O Burgo. Follow the highway downhill through Sigrás. Turn left (before a Mercadona supermarket), then right onto a footpath. Join a road uphill to the Igrexa de Santiago on the edge of

SIGRÁS (4.6KM)

Bar/Pensión La Paz (Cuesta de Alvedro 41, tel 981 650 101).

The 12th-century **Igrexa de Santiago** features a stained-glass Santiago Matamoros and medieval pilgrim hospital.

Keep straight on for 2.2km on a series of paved roads, crossing A-6/E-70 and arriving in Praza de San Marcos in **Ancéis**. Turn right onto a gravel track, then left onto a paved road. Turn left onto another gravel track and proceed 2km into **Carral** (bakery).

600 meters later, turn left onto a paved road and keep straight on for 1km, arriving at the albergue in **Sergude** (bar, **Albergue de Peregrinos** – €6, 30 beds, open all year, kitchen; **Pensión Angelita** – doubles €32–40, @, located on N-550, tel 981 671 147). The town center is just ahead. Keep straight on, then turn right onto a footpath. Rejoin a paved road and continue into

SARANDÓS (9.1KM)

Bar/grocery. **Hotel Rústico Casa das Veigas** (singles €62, doubles €72, includes breakfast, tel 981 671 616).

King Phillip II of Spain stayed at **Capilla de San Júan** while traveling to wed Mary, the English queen, in Winchester in 1554.

Keep straight on through town. Turn right onto a paved road and proceed 2.7km to **A Cruz de Beira**. Cross AE-222, then immediately turn left uphill. Continue 2.7km uphill to **As Travesas** (bar), the highest point on the Inglés (450m). Turn right onto AC 542, then left off it. Follow a path that parallels the highway, then rejoin it (and the Ferrol branch of the Inglés). After 1.2km turn left off the highway and then turn right. Continue on minor tracks into

The pilgrim fountain near O Burgo

HOSPITAL DE BRUMA (10.2KM)

See the Camino Inglés, Stage 3, for details.

For the route from Hospital de Bruma to Santiago see Camino Inglés, Stages 4 and 5.

THE RUTA DO MAR

Viveiro (Stage 4)

INTRODUCTION

Also known as the Camiño do Mar, this newly-recovered pilgrim road to Santiago offers a coastal link between the Camino del Norte and Camino Inglés. While it currently lacks the same kind of pilgrim infrastructure that its neighboring routes enjoy, its historical bonafides are clear and its spectacular coastal scenery is almost unparalleled. This is an opportunity to be a trailblazing pilgrim, away from the crowds. The stage descriptons that follow include several different route options: the Ruta do Mar proper, the Camino Natural da Ruta do Cantábrico, and the Camiño de Mañón a Santo André, along with some unnamed coastal variants. Find the walk that is right for you!

Statues outside of Viveiro's Iglesia de San Francisco

STAGE 1
Ribadeo to Praia das Catedrais

Start	Albergue de Peregrinos, Ribadeo
Finish	Praia das Catedrais
Distance	17.8km
% unpaved	48.4%
Total ascent	149m
Total descent	178m
Terrain	1
Route-finding	1
Accommodation	Ribadeo, Rinlo, Praia de Esteiro, Praia das Catedrais

The Mar begins with a highlight reel of coastal walking, with nearly the entire stage staying on or close to the ocean. Route-finding is simple, as the Ruta do Mar and Camino Cantábrico stick together throughout this stage. Rinlo offers a good opportunity for a mid-walk lunch and then the beaches begin, with a series of sandy stops leading into one of Spain's most famous beaches, Praia das Catedrais. If you're walking in summer, be sure to schedule your spot on the beach ahead of time!

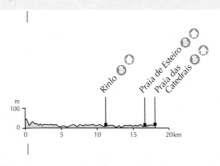

RIBADEO

All facilities. **Albergue de Peregrinos** (€6, 12 beds, kitchen, tel 659 942 159), **Albergue Ribadeo a Ponte** (€13–15, 28 beds, open all year, kitchen, W/D, @, c/Barreiro 7, tel 686 794 389), **Hotel Santa Cruz** (singles €25, doubles €40, triples €60, c/Diputación 22, tel 982 130 549), **Pensión Linares** (doubles €36+, Plaza España 13, tel 982 129 633), **Hotel Rosmary Ribadeo** (doubles €33–49, pilgrim discount, c/San Francisco 3, tel 982 128 678), **Hotel Rolle** (doubles €60–98, includes breakfast, c/Enxeñeiro Schulz 6, tel 982 120 670).

Ribadeo is the last coastal stop on the Camino del Norte, a modern development that occurred as a consequence of the highway bridge's construction – and a happy one for walkers on the Ruta do Mar who get to start their journey here. Although Ribadeo was founded by Fernando II in 1183, it was taken by the French knight Pierre de Vaillanes and not fully integrated into the larger region until the 19th century. Within the city, the **Plaza de España** features many interesting buildings, including the town hall and the 20th-century Indianos-style **Torre de los Moreno**.

A pilgrim hospital was founded in the 12th century, offering 21 beds, meals, and medical and spiritual care. The hospital was in operation in various forms until 1857 when it was sold off. Today's albergue offers million-dollar views and a perfect starting point for the Mar.

Proceed north along the coast following waymarks for the Camino Cantábrico (and occasional yellow arrows with 'CM'), passing Forte de San Damián and then looping west past **Faro Illa Pancha**. After a short inland digression, the majority of the route is right along the coast.

RINLO (11.1KM)

Bars/restaurants. **Hotel Porto de Rinlo** (doubles €40+, meals available, @, Plaza Santa Catalina 9, tel 982 123 137), **Hotel Mi Norte** (singles €50–102, doubles €60–111, tel 667 404 556) located near the train station.

The **Igrexa de San Pedro** is a neo-Gothic structure, dating to the early 20th century. The **Cetárea de Rinlo**, just after town, was one of Spain's earliest shellfish farms dating to 1904.

Leave Rinlo along the coast, passing the **Cetárea de Rinlo**. The Praia dos Castros (**bar, toilets/fountain**) marks the beginning of a series of beaches, followed by Praia das Illas and then

The first kilometer of the Camino Cantábrico

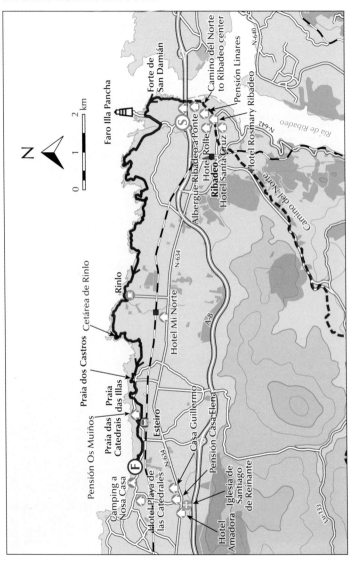

PRAIA DE ESTEIRO (5.6KM)

Café/Pensión Os Muiños (doubles €65, meals available, tel 982 156 113). Esteiro train station is just south of here.

Continue straight, following the paved road, dirt track, and wooden promenade to

PRAIA DAS CATEDRAIS (1.1KM)

Bars/restaurants, tourist information kiosk at end of beach in high season. Accommodation options at the neighboring Praia Arealonga: **Hotel Playa de las Catedrales** (doubles €45–85, triples/quads, open late-May–early-Oct, meals available, @, tel 982 134 012), **Camping a Nosa Casa** (doubles €60, includes breakfast, bungalows with kitchen €60–75 (2–3 people) or €80–100 (4 people), café, W/D, tel 982 134 005). Options 2km south of the beach: **Casa Guillermo** (doubles €39–64, open all year, includes breakfast, kitchen, laundry service, @, tel 982 134 150), **Pensión Casa Elena** (doubles €40–65, open all year, breakfast available, laundry service, @, tel 982 134 087), **Hotel Amadora** (doubles €50–60, meals available, Crta General Reinante 6, tel 982 134 044).

One of Spain's most famous beaches, with the 'cathedrals' in the name referring to the dramatic cliffs, arches, and caves that emerge at low tide. Reservations are required from July to September to help manage crowd size. It's free – go to: ascatedrais.xunta.gal.

The coast near Praia das Catedrais

STAGE 2
Praia das Catedrais to Foz

Start	Praia das Catedrais
Finish	Port of Foz
Distance	21.8km
% unpaved	8.6%
Total ascent	357m
Total descent	369m
Terrain	2
Route-finding	4
Accommodation	On recommended route – Praia de Fontela, Punta San Bartolo, A Espiñeira, Vilaronte, Foz. On alternative routes – San Cosme de Barreiros

The route becomes more complicated today, as the Mar and Cantábrico split immediately after Catedrais and rarely overlap. Our preferred route is to follow the Cantábrico through the first 9.6km, wrapping around the coast and the eastern side of the Ría de Foz, and then after joining the Mar to cross the Río Masma and remain with the Mar as it forks away from the Cantábrico toward A Espiñeira. This leads to the day's major highlight – the Basílica de San Martiño de Mondoñedo. The oldest (former) cathedral in Spain, the basilica has some outstanding murals and merits a long visit. From there, we suggest following a direct approach to Foz, which has many accommodation options.

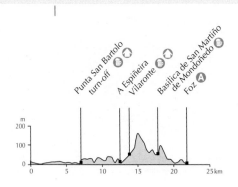

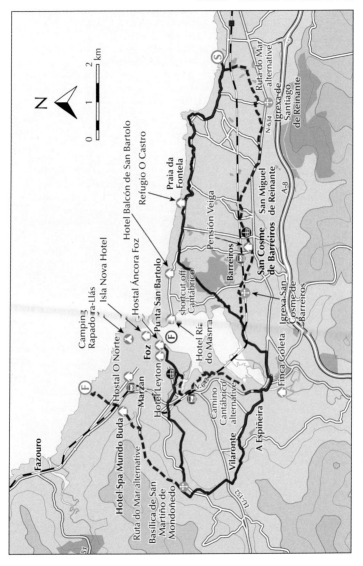

Cantábrico waymarks in this opening section are consistent and reliable. The route generally follows rock walkways along the coastline, passing a series of fantastic beaches, including **Praia da Fontela** (bar/restaurant, **Refugio O Castro** – doubles €45–140, includes breakfast, @, tel 982 124 150). At Playa Remior (**bar**), arrive at

PUNTA SAN BARTOLO TURNOFF (7.2KM)

We recommend a shortcut here, turning left on an unmarked road and reconnecting with the Cantábrico near San Cosme. This lops 2.1km off the walk. Alternatively, those who wish to remain on the Cantábrico can find bars, restaurants, and accommodation 0.5–1km further west in Punta San Bartolo, including **Hotel Balcón de San Bartolo** (doubles €45–140, tel 982 124 226) and **Hotel Ría do Masma** (singles €20–30, doubles €30–40, open all year, breakfast available, tel 982 124 085).

The remains of many Iron Age-era settlements, or *castros*, are evident along the coast in this stretch. The **Castro de San Bartolo** is representative of those remains, with a stone path leading out to a mostly overgrown peninsula, with the coastal edges of the old settlement gradually being eroded by the sea.

Mar waymarks are inconsistent and unreliable – watch the map carefully.

Soon after the shortcut and the Camino Cantábrico rejoin, the Mar also arrives from the left, bringing all routes together for the crossing of the Río Masma (**restaurant**). ◄ The Mar forks left at the second turn after the river, leading into

A ESPIÑEIRA (5.6KM)

Bar. **Finca Goleta** (doubles €80, triples €96, tel 687 854 290), located just south after crossing the Río Masma.

Follow the highway northwest, forking off to the left shortly before arrival in

VILARONTE (1.3KM)

Casa da Roxa (doubles €40+, includes breakfast, tel 982 137 161).

The **Igrexa de San Xoán de Vilaronte** is one block off-route.

Basílica de San Martiño de Mondoñedo

Cross two minor highways, pass through a short wooded stretch, and then cross a third minor highway before proceeding into

BASÍLICA DE SAN MARTIÑO DE MONDOÑEDO (3.3KM)

Bar/restaurant.

Celtic Christians, known as Bretons, fled the British Isles to the Iberian Peninsula around 560 and then relocated to this area in the early ninth century. The basilica's original construction likely dates to that time, although other claims point

83

to the sixth century; the current Romanesque structure dates to the 12th century. It is believed to be the oldest cathedral in Spain, consecrated by Bishop San Rosendo in 925. The cathedral seat was moved inland to Valibria in the 12th century to protect it from sea raids; to honor this basilica, Valibria changed its name to Mondoñedo. The Camino del Norte passes through there and the two Mondoñedos are linked by the **Camiño Natural de San Rosendo**, which is a way-marked trail that spans 27km.

The current basilica was raised by Bishop Gonzalo, who is credited with destroying the Norman fleet that was raiding the coast, through repeated prayer.

When only a few ships remained, he let them go to warn others from attacking these shores. The basilica has many architectural highlights, including its 11 surviving, evocative capitals, and particularly the ones surrounding the transept. More notably, it preserves its original murals, restored in 2007 and dating to the 12th century, on the transept's south side. These narrate the stories of the Tree of Jesse, the Assumption of Mary, and the Salvation of the Righteous. Other paintings exist in more deteriorated states on other walls, including the narrative of the three magi and the resurrection of Lazarus. Note that the basilica is closed on Mondays (open 1000–1300, 1600–2000, Tue–Sun).

Original painting preserved in the Basílica de San Martiño de Mondoñedo

The neighboring **Botanical Garden Espazo Caritel** combines a small art museum, featuring ceramics and a photo exhibit by artist Daniel Caxigueiro, with a botanical garden that includes native and exotic plants, featuring magnolias, hydrangeas, and camellias. It's also closed Mondays (open 1130–1400, 1700–2030 Tue–Sat, 1130–1400 Sun).

While the Mar continues straight past the basilica, this route bypasses the town of Foz. To reach the town center, instead turn right immediately after the basilica, then left on LU-2001. Don't expect any waymarks in this stretch. Follow a series of roads 3.6km, ultimately rejoining the Camino Cantábrico at a football pitch, shortly before arrival in

FOZ (4.4KM)

All facilities. **Hostel Áncora Foz** (beds €20, @, Mestre Mateo 8, tel 982 132 410), **Hotel Leyton** (singles €30–50, doubles €50–70, open all year, includes breakfast, @, Avda da Mariña 6, tel 982 140 800), **Isla Nova Hotel** (singles €49–70, doubles €70–92, triples €92–114, closed Dec holiday, breakfast available, @, c/ Emilia Pardo Bazán 7, tel 982 133 606), **Hotel Spa Mundo Buda** (doubles €60–110, includes breakfast and spa, Crta de Forxan 30, tel 628 011 672), **Camping Rapadoira-Llás** (caravan rentals €55–65, laundry and café/grocery on-site, @, tel 982 140 713), **Hostal O Norte** (singles €30–45, doubles €40–65, triples €50–80, meals available, Avda Viveiro 49, tel 982 132 181).

A whaling post and important shipyard in the 16th and 17th centuries, Foz enjoys a lively port and busy downtown core. Its deep connection to the sea is reflected in local culinary specialities such as grilled sardines, fried chinchos, octopus with clams, hake, and bispo stew. One of the largest marine bird colonies in Northwest Spain is located in the neighboring marshland. Its **Igrexa de Santiago** is a 16th-century structure with two altarpieces, one rococo and the other neo-classical. Foz is the antipode of Christchurch, New Zealand.

Foz from across the bay

85

Ruta do Mar alternative, from Praia das Catedrais to San Cosme de Barreiros

Leave Praia das Catedrais on the Camino Cantábrico, following a wooden boardwalk. One block later, the routes split, with yellow arrows calling for a left turn – follow these inland. Shortly before reaching N-634, the route heads west and generally proceeds between N-634 and the railroad over the next stretch, with a couple of brief exceptions, passing through the neighborhood of **San Miguel de Reinante** (bars/restaurants) and then continuing into

SAN COSME DE BARREIROS (6.4KM)

Bar/restaurant, supermarket. Barreiros train station. **Pensión Veiga** (doubles €40–60, triples €70–90, @, tel 982 124 241), **Hotel A Finca** (doubles €60–70, quads €110–120, includes breakfast, @, tel 982 124 611).

This region is rich in Indianos-style architecture, a trend associated with Spaniards who acquired wealth in the 'New World' and then returned to Galicia (or other parts of Spain). Look for large windows, bright colors, and accompanying gardens, often with palm trees. The **Igrexa de San Cosme de Barreiros** is a 17th- to 18th-century single-nave structure with a baroque altarpiece.

The Camino Cantábrico joins soon after the **Igrexa de San Cosme de Barreiros**, coming in from the right. This route is 1km shorter than the Cantábrico with the shortcut, or 3.1km shorter than the Cantábrico in its entirety, and almost entirely on pavement.

Camino Cantábrico alternative, from the Río Masma to Foz

After the Mar turns left, continue along N-642 for 600 meters before turning right onto a minor paved road. The route ultimately winds back to N-642 near the Foz train station before cutting inland on a waymarked footpath. Soon after, the Cantábrico passes a football pitch, with the route from Mondoñedo joining from the left. Continue into the center of **Foz**. This route is

4.2km shorter than the recommended approach past the basilica.

Ruta do Mar alternative bypassing Foz center

The 'official' Mar continues straight past the **Basílica de San Martiño de Mondoñedo**, following a series of minor roads 2.2km to the Capela do Bispo Santo and its neighboring park. Pass left around the chapel and park, then arrive at another intersection, where you face another important decision. Continue straight to reach the coast, 1.9km later, where you can reconnect with the Camino Cantábrico on Foz's far western outskirts (4.6km from the port). Alternatively, turn left to remain on the 'official' Mar. Be warned, however, that this route doesn't provide any opportunity for provision until Cangas (9.2km), nor any chance at accommodation until Burela (14.8km). Note that **Hotel Spa Mundo Buda** is mere meters downhill from this split, along the road toward the coast.

A cruceiro near the basilica

STAGE 3
Foz to San Cibrao

Start	Port of Foz
Finish	Casa da Cultura, San Cibrao
Distance	32.8km
% unpaved	19.2%
Total ascent	538m
Total descent	532m
Terrain	2
Route-finding	4
Accommodation	On recommended route at Burela, Cervo, San Cibrao

This is a longer walk, but one offering outstanding variety and some notable cultural highlights. As was true yesterday, we recommend spending your morning on the Cantábrico, following the coast from Foz to Burela, before veering inland on the Mar in the afternoon. Burela offers a fantastic spot for lunch or supplies, with many restaurants and supermarkets, while the walk to Sargadelos is quite memorable, with a small arboretum, a lovely historic park, and a shady trail following the river into Cervo. San Cibrao is a highlight as well: a small town perched on a peninsula jutting into the sea, with deep, sandy beaches unfolding toward the gently lapping waves.

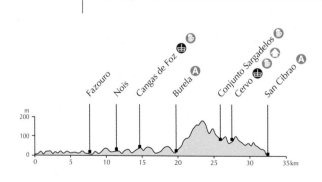

Leaving Foz, return to the port and follow the Cantábrico's rock pedestrian track out of town. Pass a series of excellent beaches, including the Rapadoira, Llas, and Peizas. Divert inland, passing under N-642 in order to reach a pedestrian bridge across the Río do Ouro at the entrance to Fazouro, 7.9km after leaving Foz.

Continue on the Cantábrico into **Fazouro**, turning right immediately after the bridge. ▶ The Cantábrico returns promptly to the coast, passing the **Castro de Fazouro** soon after. The second-century BC castro is one of the best to visit on the Mar, fully excavated and well preserved. Continue to the Igrexa de Nois in

You could turn left here to join the Mar, passing a Santiago Peregrino sculpture close to the Igrexa de Santiago, and take the next right turn.

NOIS (11.3KM)

Train station and pharmacy near N-642.

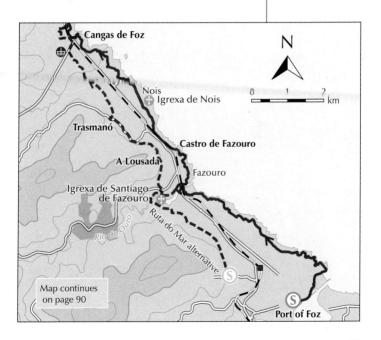

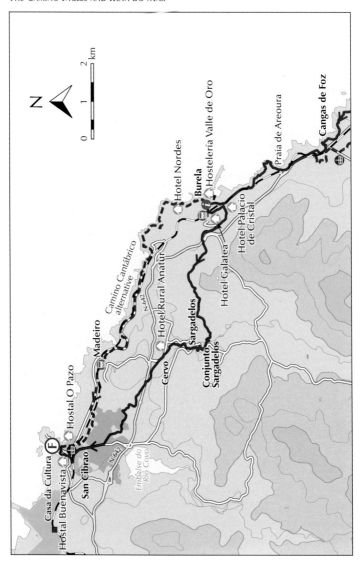

Another section of coastal walking leads to another parish church in

CANGAS DE FOZ (3.4KM)

Bar and supermarket located across N-642.

The 16th-century **Igrexa de San Pedro de Cangas de Foz** enjoys a glorious position on a small ridge overlooking the sea. Its Capilla do Carmen features an acclaimed altarpiece.

The Mar joins from the left soon after Cangas. After a short stint running parallel to N-642, the Cantábrico forks right back onto the coast, wrapping around the **Praia de Areoura** (toilets, bar). While the route has been disrupted by significant road construction projects, at this point it likely follows the coast into the port of

BURELA (5KM)

All facilities, mostly clustered uphill around Avda Arcadio Pardiñas. **Hotel Galatea** (singles €30–50, doubles €45–70, family €70–120, open all year, includes breakfast, @, tel 655 961 636), **Hotel Nordes** (singles €37–44, doubles €44–66, Avda da Mariña 57, tel 982 575 143), **Hotel Palacio de Cristal** (singles €36, doubles €53, breakfast available, Avda Arcadio Pardiñas 154, tel 982 585 803), **Hostería Valle de Oro** (tel 982 580 080). Small turismo in port.

First documented in 1096, Burela's history has focused on agriculture, livestock, and fishing, but the precious 'Torques of Burela' speak to an early goldsmithing wave. Whaling emerged as the key industry in the Middle Ages, but the decline of white whales in the 18th century caused a recession that lasted until the late-19th century. The bonito and hake catch are big today.

Burela's **Barco Museo 'Reina del Carmen'** (Tue–Sat, 1100–1300, 1700–1900, €5) is housed in an actual boat built in Burela in 1968, used for swordfish and hake fishing in the Atlantic, and retired in 1998. The **Iglesia de Santa María's** nave features paintings of Jesus's life. It had been abandoned, exposed, and overgrown, but the parish priest and community rallied to repair/restore it. The **Igrexa da Vila do Medio**, meanwhile, has an excellent set of 16th-century murals, featuring six scenes from the life of Jesus.

Yellow arrow waymarks exist once you leave town, but in many cases they are faded or overgrown. Look in particular at the base of electrical/telephone poles.

We recommend following the Mar from Burela. ◄ Turn left from the port onto Rúa de Eijo Garay and proceed uphill. While there's some backtracking involved, it's possible to minimize this by continuing straight across Avda de Arcadio Pardiñas and then turning right on Rúa San Román de Vilaestrofe. After crossing N-642, turn right, skirting the edge of the village of **Sargadelos** (its Igrexa de Santiago is a neoclassical structure with a 17th-century Santiago Peregrino) before descending through a small arboretum and arriving at the

CONJUNTO HISTÓRICO ARTÍSTICO DE SARGADELOS (6.1KM)

Bar.

Galician industrialization began here in 1791 with the first blast furnaces devoted to iron next to mines that generated iron, kaolin, and quartz. The Marquis of Sargadelos founded the factory, but faced a mutiny among the peasants in 1798 and the destruction of his factories; he was then murdered in 1809.

Undeterred, Antonio Raimundo Ibáñez founded the Sargadelos factory here in 1806. Ibáñez was a key force in Galician industrialization, developing new sea trade routes and an ironworks factory, and producing ammunition for the government (as well as kitchen utensils, hydraulic wheels, and public sculptures and fountains). Then, he capitalized on nearby clay deposits and the interruption of trade with Britain to launch the porcelain factory here. By the 1830s, the factory was producing up to 20,000 pieces annually; it reached its golden age in 1849, with 1000 families working for the factory. However, decline soon followed, as a result of internal disputes among the owning family (and accompanying lawsuits), resulting in the company shutting down in 1875. The perimeter walls of the old factory were declared a historic-artistic monument nearly a century later, in 1972. Around the same time, in 1968, the Sargadelos company was re-established, restoring the prominent role of ceramic production in Galicia. It has a gallery on the outskirts of Cervo and another in Santiago de Compostela.

The surrounding park is wooded and peaceful, at the confluence of the Xunco and Rúa rivers, with a botanical path gathering native arboreal species of Galicia around Monte Escarabelada.

Conjunto Histórico Artístico de Sargadelos

A lovely walk follows the waymarked 'Camino Real' and 'Sendeiro Peonil for Ruta Sargadelos' through a wooded stretch along the Río Xunco into

CERVO (1.6KM)

Grocery, bar. **Hotel Rural Anatur** offers high-quality rooms but may require a two-night stay (tel 692 646 000).

The **Museo Histórico de Sargadelos** (Tue–San, 1030–1400, 1600–1900, free) documents the history of the original Sargadelos ceramics factory, located in the old complex's administrative house, while the **Sargadelos Galería de Cervo** (Mon–Fri 0930–2000, Sat–Sun 1100–1400, 1600–2000) would be happy to fill your pack with their current offerings. The **Igrexa de Santa María** is a baroque structure with a medieval baptismal font.

This final stretch is road-bound, passing along highways and through quiet suburbs before a last descent leads to the western edge of San Cibrao's peninsula. Turn right, rejoining the Cantábrico, and backtracking into the center of

SAN CIBRAO (5.4KM)

Bars, restaurants, supermarket. **Hostal Buenavista** (singles €24–36, doubles €40–55, triples €55–60, meals available in summer, @, tel 982 594 086), **Hostal O Pazo** (tel 982 594 066), **Hotel O Castelo** (doubles €38–55, open all year, meals available, laundry service, @, tel 982 594 402, located on the camino 2.7km after San Cibrao).

Despite San Cibrao's outstanding beaches, tourism remains a modest part of an economy more reliant on fisheries and the nearby aluminum plant. A mermaid statue on the beach corresponds to a local legend of a siren, La Maruxaina, who lives on the Os Farallons islands near San Cibrao. Public perception of the mermaid was split – some claimed that she helped save sailors, while others accused her of cruelty and deception. During the Maruxaina festival, on the second Saturday in August, the mermaid is put on trial on the beach (an enviable courtroom!). While she is always found guilty, fear not – a pardon quickly follows, along with singing, dancing, and the traditional Galician *queimada* (a flaming alcoholic beverage, prepared with incantation).

The **Capela de San Cibrao** dates to the 12th century at least, although the carved stone bar is believed to be eighth/ninth century and may have been used to baptize the first Christians of San Cibrao. The altarpiece is strikingly colourful. The **Museo Provincial do Mar** (Tue–Sat 1100–1400, 1700–2000, Sun 1100–1400, free) is Galicia's oldest public museum, narrating the history of San Cibrao and Galicia's relationship with the sea.

The beach in San Cibrao

Ruta do Mar alternative, from Fazouro to Cangas de Foz

Those who chose to follow the Mar from San Martiño do Mondoñedo will have already walked 7.7km when this route joins from Fazouro. Those coming from the Cantábrico face a 500-meter detour on the Camiño Ponte de Ferro to link the two routes, connecting near the Igrexa de Santiago de Fazouro.

The Mar has few advantages over the Cantábrico in this stretch, generally following paved roads with decent coastal views all the way to Cangas de Foz. It passes through the villages of **A Lousada** (1km) and **Trasmanó** (1.5km) before turning right on LU-162 toward **Cangas de Foz**, passing a supermarket and bar. After skirting the edge of town, the Mar joins the Cantábrico soon after crossing the railroad. This route is roughly equivalent in length to the recommended approach. The waymarking is poor.

Camino Cantábrico alternative, from Burela to San Cibrao

This is one of the Cantábrico's less rewarding stretches, with the majority of the coastline screened off by the railroad. Departure from Burela is excellent, as the route passes directly alongside a series of beaches in quick succession – the Portelo, Ril, and Marosa. However, after that there is little to highlight; the most notable landmark is the train station in **Madeiro**, some 7.8km from Burela. Ultimately, the route brings you to the east side of San Cibrao's peninsula. Turn left inland at the end of Caosa beach and proceed directly on Rúa da Caosa to the **Casa da Cultura**. This route spans 11km from Burela, making it 2km shorter than the recommended route.

STAGE 4
San Cibrao to Viveiro

Start	Casa da Cultura, San Cibrao
Finish	Office of Tourism, Viveiro
Distance	29.7km
% unpaved	44.2%
Total ascent	832m
Total descent	833m
Terrain	4
Route-finding	3
Accommodation	Area, Celeiro, Viveiro (and Covas)

The Cantábrico and Mar follow similar arcs today, looping around the Costa da Mariña Occidental, although the Mar cuts inland at several points instead of adhering to the coastline. We recommend sticking with the Cantábrico, but if 30km is too much, the Mar offers a few opportunities to trim some distance. A bar outside of San Cibrao offers a good early breakfast opportunity; from that point on, however, chances for food are very limited, so stock up before leaving San Cibrao. The walk generally proceeds along rugged coastal terrain, with beaches at the beginning and end. Viveiro is another Mar highlight: a vibrant town loaded with stunning examples of Galician architecture.

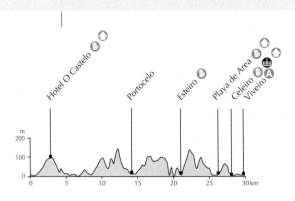

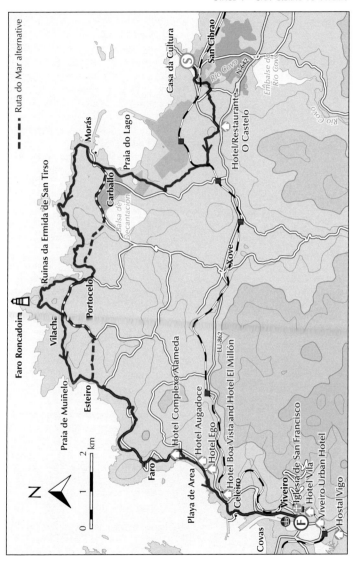

Throughout this walk, Cantábrico waymarks are excellent, while Mar yellow arrows are present at key turns, but spotty at all other points.

◄ Leaving San Cibrao, this stage starts with a lovely wooded stretch alongside the Río Covo, before emerging at a bar (open surprisingly early!) near N-642 and **Hotel O Castelo**. The route proceeds through a series of industrial facilities, before arriving at a route split just after the Praia do Lago, 7.6km from San Cibrao. We recommend sticking with the Camino Cantábrico along the coast here, as we do all day. The Cantábrico swings northeastward along the coast, skirting the village and port of **Morás** before wrapping back to the west. This is a stunning stretch of coastline, with little traffic or development, leading eventually back to LU-2607 (the Mar joins from the left) and then descending into

PORTOCELO (14.1KM)

Toilets and fountain at beach.

Soon after passing the beach's western access point, the Mar and Cantábrico split once again. Forking right with the Cantábrico offers superior coastal views and a good amount of off-road walking. The route proceeds to the **Ruinas da Ermida de San Tirso**. According to legend, San Tirso's body arrived on a stone boat at the foot of the cliff beneath the hermitage, and that boat is said to be visible at low tide. The chapel was founded by Rodrigo of Coimbra, an eighth-century deacon who fled here away from the Moorish invasion, and built upon ruins of an Iron Age castro. Continue past the access point for the Faro Roncadoira, skirt the edge of **Vilachá**, and then swing wide to the west, rejoining the Mar above **Praia de Muiñelo** and just before the descent into

ESTEIRO (6.8KM)

Bar/restaurant, toilets and fountain at beach.

The beach is popular with surfers, with large sand dunes and little surrounding development.

From here, the Cantábrico and Mar appear to sync up (with one small exception), but there is a dearth of yellow arrows. Between Esteiro and **Playa de Area**, the route generally follows LU-2610, but it swings widely to the left and right at different points, before ultimately returning. After passing through **Faro** and its Antigua Igrexa de San Xiao, tracks lead downhill to the stunning

Playa de Esteiro

PLAYA DE AREA (5.2KM)

Bars, restaurant. **Hotel Ego** (singles €77–110, doubles €100–143, breakfast available, tel 982 560 987), **Hotel Complexo Alameda** (doubles €58–95, includes breakfast, @, tel 982 551 088), **Hotel Augadoce** (doubles, meals available, @, tel 982 560 944).

Arguably the nicest beach in the area, with calm waters, soft sand, and abundant neighboring vegetation, with a nearby island that houses a marine bird refuge. It is joined in the area by the ruins of the Roman town of Estáñón and the medieval village of Arenas.

A short climb leads to an equivalent drop, leading to the most 'urban' stretch of the day through the busy port town of

CELEIRO (1.9KM)

Bars/restaurants, grocery, bakery. **Hotel Boa Vista** (singles €35–55, doubles €49–80, meals available, @, tel 982 562 290), **Hotel El Millón** (singles €25–30, doubles €35–50, meals available, @, tel 982 561 191).

A pilgrim hospital operated here in the Middle Ages, funded by the bishop of Mondoñedo. Coastal monuments are devoted to 'the castaway' and the Virgen del Carmen. The town's most notable building, the headquarters of the fishermen's collective, is named in honor of Santiago.

It's all road from here, proceeding from the port of Celeiro to N-642 and then following the highway to the turismo in

VIVEIRO (1.7KM)

All facilities. **Hotel Vila** (singles €25–32, doubles €35–60, breakfast available, @, tel 982 561 331), **Hostal Vigo** (tel 982 562 286), **Viveiro Urban Hotel** (singles €55–60, doubles €60–70, breakfast available, @, tel 982 562 101).

This town has ancient origins, reflected in prehistoric megaliths, castro settlements, and Roman ruins. The earliest documented evidence of Viveiro dates to 857, but it fully blossomed in the 12th century, once Norman and Muslim threats dissipated. Small bits of the old town wall survive, most notably the 16th-century **Castelo da Ponte**, featuring imperial arms of Carlos V. The **Praza Maior** is a hub of marvellous examples of Galician architecture, reshaped in the 19th century following the collapse of the parish Igrexa de Santiago and the elimination of the old prison. The **Callejón del Muro** is among the narrowest streets in Spain. Viveiro's **Ponte Maior**, which you will cross leaving town, dates to 1225, although the current structure was initiated in 1462.

Viveiro has numerous historic religious structures. Its **Iglesia de San Francisco** was originally part of a Franciscan convent founded in 1219, but the surviving church is of the 14th century. The **Iglesia de Santa María** is a 12th-century Romanesque structure and features a set of corbels devoted to lust and other sins. Finally, the **Convento de las Concepcionistas** has a replica of the Lourdes grotto with many wax offerings of gratitude for healing miracles.

Viveiro is known for one of Galicia's major Semana Santa celebrations, supported by seven different local 'brotherhoods' responsible for coordinating and funding events.

Ruta do Mar alternative, from before Morás to the Praia de Muiñelo

Shortly after the **Praia do Lago**, yellow arrows call for a left turn onto a dirt track and then another left, back-tracking on LU-2602. The Mar then heads west, gently uphill, passing through the village of **Carballo** (bar) and to the right of a 'lake' (you'll be happiest if you don't look in). Rejoin the Cantábrico 3km later, looping through **Portocelo**. When the route splits after 1km, fork left to remain on LU-2607. Arrive in **Vilachá** 1.1km later, with its church just off-route to the left. After arriving at a T-junction with LU-2610, turn right and then immediately right again, onto a dirt track. This brings you to the coast, where you'll rejoin the Cantábrico, turning left to continue. This route spans 7.5km, making it 4.8km shorter than the recommended approach

Historic Viviero

STAGE 5
Viveiro to Cuiña

Start	Office of Tourism, Viveiro
Finish	Iglesia de Santiago, Cuiña
Distance	31.2km (alternative 55.1km)
% unpaved	26.6%
Total ascent	1054m
Total descent	1052m
Terrain	5
Route-finding	5
Accommodation	Covas, Couzadoiro, Cuiña (alternative – O Vicedo, Porto do Barqueiro, Ortigueira)

Will this be one stage for you, or two? Our recommended approach, following the Mar almost due west across the base of the peninsula, is efficient and historic, and also quite rural. Aside from a few minor villages, you will encounter little sign of habitation along this walk and certainly no opportunities for food between Covas and Cuiña. The most notable development in this stretch is the emergence of waymarks for the local pilgrimage to San Andrés de Teixido after crossing the Ponte do Porto; these stone balises will continue to be a presence in your walk not only to San Andrés, but also onward to Ferrol, as the route is marked in both directions. Alternatively, you can follow the Cantábrico along the coast which will nearly double your walk but the scenery is worth the trouble. Note that the Cantábrico concludes just before Ortigueira, in Ladrido, so be prepared to follow the map carefully from there.

Cross the Ponte Maior out of Viveiro and then follow the coastal promenade into

COVAS (2.9KM)

Bars/restaurants, supermarket, pharmacy. **Hotel Las Sirenas** (singles €40–60, doubles €45–70, meals available, tel 982 560 200), **Hotel Celta Galaico** (doubles €38–45, triples €60–74, open Mar-Oct, breakfast available, tel 982 550 800),

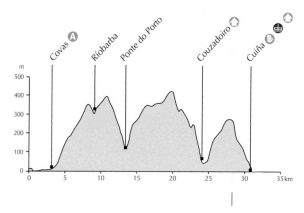

Hotel As Areas (doubles €37–49, triples €49–59, tel 982 560 605), **Hotel Dolusa** (singles €45, doubles €60–69, tel 982 560 866).

This narrow town lines the expansive Playa de Covas. A monument on the west-side commemorates the 'naúfragos' of the Cantabrian squad, which sank here in 1810. The **Igrexa de San Juan de Covas** dates to the 18th century and features a baroque altarpiece.

▸ Cut inland past **Hotel Las Sirenas** and continue westward through a roundabout on LU-P-6603. Some 1.5km from Covas, the Cantábrico forks right, but continue straight on the highway to

Mar waymarks in this section are sorely lacking.

RÍOBARBA (6.7KM)

No facilities.

The **Igrexa de San Pablo de Ríobarba** was built in the late-14th century by Fernán Pérez de Andrade, the same man responsible for the bridge in Pontedeume and many other structures in Galicia. The 15th-century murals of Saint Paul survive within.

Some 900 meters after Ríobarba, just after a sharp bend to the right, fork left at an unmarked intersection.

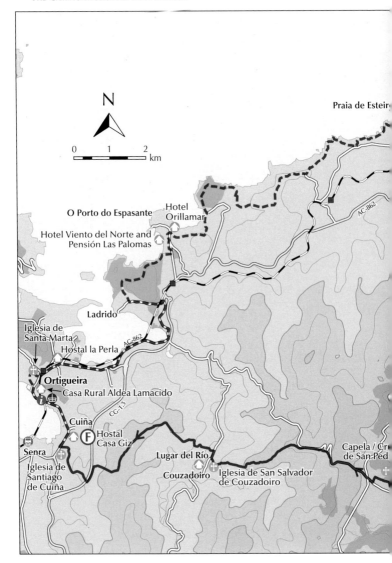

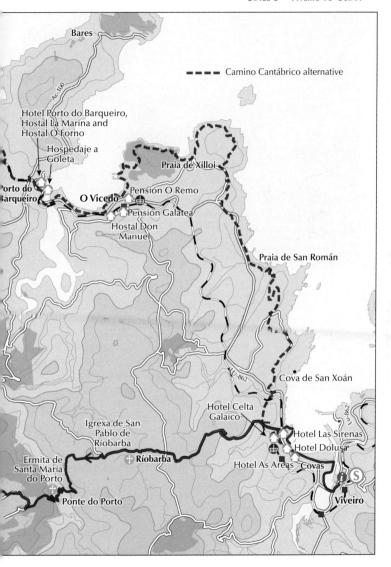

- - - - Camino Cantábrico alternative

Bares

Hotel Porto do Barqueiro,
Hostal La Marina and
Hostal O Forno

Hospedaje a
Goleta

Porto do
Barqueiro

O Vicedo

Pensión O Remo

Praia de Xilloi

Pensión Galatea

Hostal Don
Manuel

Praia de San Román

Cova de San Xoán

Hotel Celta
Galaico

Igrexa de San
Pablo de
Ríobarba

Hotel Las Sirenas

Hotel Dolusa

Ríobarba

Hotel As Areas

Covas

Ermita de
Santa María
do Porto

Viveiro

Ponte do Porto

The Ponte do Porto marks the end of a sustained descent and the beginning of a sharp climb

This winds 3km downhill to the **Ponte do Porto**, a bridge of medieval origins that was a critical link on the Viveiro-Ortigueira road. It is preceded by the **Ermita de Santa María do Porto**. From there, the ascent begins, switch-backing up to a height equivalent to that from which you just descended, leading 4.8km to the **Capela and Cruz de San Pedro**. Return to DP-4402, watching for two critical opportunities to fork left onto a footpath. The second is particularly critical, leading downhill into

COUZADOIRO (14.5KM)

Lugar del Río (doubles €65, quad €100, includes breakfast, open Mar–Oct, W/D, @, tel 680 766 819).

There are two parish churches in close proximity here: the **Iglesia de San Cristobal de Couzadoiro**, a baroque structure with an image of the Black Virgin of Loreto within, and the **Iglesia de San Salvador de Couzadoiro**, which has a fountain out front.

Follow minor roads and occasional dirt tracks through wooded terrain, eventually crossing the Costa Norte highway and arriving soon after in

CUIÑA (7.1KM)

Bar/restaurant. **Hostal Casa Giz** (singles €25, doubles €42–49, @, tel 981 400 873) also has a restaurant and small grocery. Senra train station is 1.2km away.

The **Igrexa de Santiago de Cuiña** is one block south of where the route crosses AC-862.

Camino Cantábrico alternative, from Covas to Cuiña
After splitting from the Mar shortly after **Covas**, the Cantábrico proceeds northward on pleasant trails through the woods. Some 1.5km later, arrive at the turnoff for Cova de San Xoán, the site of a local pilgrimage. Legend goes that a man with white hair and beard, dressed in a robe with a staff, appeared here on the night of Saint John's day. Speculation followed that it was indeed Saint John; since that appearance, claims exist that no shipwrecks occurred in the area. A chapel was built in the nearby cave after the apparition, although it was replaced by a newer one in 1738. In the walk that follows, the Cantábrico alternates stretches on minor highways with quality off-road sections, leading 6.1km to **Praia de San Román** (restaurant) and 7km more to **Praia de Xilloi** (restaurant) before arriving in

O VICEDO (20.3KM)

Bars/restaurants, supermarket. **Pensión O Remo** (singles €20–30, doubles €30–40, triples €40–50, open all year, @, tel 982 590 202), **Hostal Don Manuel** (singles €35, doubles €55, meals available, laundry, @, tel 982 590 355), **Pensión Galatea** (singles €20, doubles €30–35, @, tel 982 590 508).

This is a modest town with a small port, flanked on the west by the expansive **Praia de Arealonga**.

After following the coastline out of town, join a track through a narrow, wooded stretch alongside the Praia de Arealonga. Cross the Río Sor and then follow another track northward past the O Barqueiro train station and into

PORTO DO BARQUEIRO (4.2KM)

Bars/restaurants, supermarket, bakery. **Hotel Porto do Barqueiro** (doubles €40–60, @, tel 981 414 134), **Hostal La Marina** (doubles €30–40, tel 981 414 098), **Hostal O Forno** (singles €25–35, doubles €35–50, triples €50–65, tel 981 414 124), **Hospedaje a Goleta** (doubles €25–60, meals available, @, tel 981 424 002).

Named for the ferry that used to cross the river before the bridge's construction in 1901, this small town is packed tightly around the port and the Ría del Barquero, an estuary that forms the mouth of the Río Sor and marks the border between the Galician provinces of Lugo and A Coruña. The northernmost point of the Iberian Peninsula is 7km (by car) away in Estaca de Bares.

Cut inland, briefly joining the AC-862 as it curves sharply left, and then turn right, passing the cemetery on your left soon after. After following the railroad away from town, cross over, wrap around the **Praia de Esteiro**, and join the coastline. This is excellent walking, mostly on unpaved pedestrian tracks, to the peninsular settlement of

O PORTO DO ESPASANTE (15.2KM)

Bars/restaurants, supermarket, bakery. **Hotel Viento del Norte** (singles €45–60, doubles €69–120, breakfast available, @, tel 981 408 182), **Pensión Las Palomas** (singles €40–45, doubles €50–60, includes breakfast, @, tel 981 408 311), **Hotel Orillamar** (doubles €60–65, quads €70–75, includes breakfast, @, tel 981 408 014).

O Porto do Espasante is a typical fishing village surrounded by three beaches – the Concha, San Antonio, and Santa Cristina. Its **Mirador de la Casa de A Vela** is situated in an 18th-century military post, offering fantastic views of Cape Ortegal and Estaca de Bares. The nearby **Castro de Punta dos Prados** is well-preserved, with some excellent remains of domestic quarters, including heated baths.

The last bit of the Cantábrico leads southwest, looping 3.5km into the small town of **Ladrido** (Pensión Bajamar – doubles €30–50, tel 981 408 063). From here to Ortigueira, you're on your own, but it's straightforward enough. Head east out of town, then turn right onto AC-862 and follow it directly to

ORTIGUEIRA (10KM)

All facilities. **Hostal la Perla** (doubles, @, tel 981 400 150), **Casa Rural Aldea Lamacido** (doubles €55, meals available, tel 981 418 814). Turismo at the end of town.

Ortigueira is famous for its international festival of Celtic music each July. The 18th-century **Igrexa de Santa Marta**, built in a neoclassical style, is part of the old Dominican convent complex. The altarpiece features Santo Domingo at the top, with Santa Rosa de Lima, Santa Catalina, San Pedro Martír, and San Francisco de Asís beneath.

After cutting inland through town, passing by the church and joining the waterfront, return to AC-862 and proceed 2.5km into **Cuiña**, rejoining the Mar.

Waymarks for the Teixido pilgrimage emerge on this stage

STAGE 6
Cuiña to Teixido

Start	Iglesia de Santiago, Cuiña
Finish	Iglesia de San Andrés de Teixido
Distance	20.9km (alternative 38.2km)
% unpaved	24.9%
Total ascent	669m
Total descent	542m
Terrain	4
Route-finding	4
Accommodation	The closest option en route is roughly 10km further on in San Román de Montoxo (alternative – Féas, A Pedra, Cariño).

While the Cantábrico has concluded, fear not – you once again have the ability to choose between the direct Mar and a coastal variant that spans nearly twice the distance. For the first time, the Mar is the more reliably waymarked option, even if that's damning with faint praise, and largely a consequence of the balises linked to the San Andrés de Teixido pilgrimage. Indeed, today is all about Teixido, a shrine of great religious significance, preceded by some of the most dramatic cliffs in the Iberian Peninsula. Our suggested approach is following the direct Mar route, but those with time will enjoy the exceptionally rugged views of the Cabo Ortegal between Cariño and Teixido. Note that accommodation is not available in Teixido, so plan to either taxi into Cedeira for the night or walk onto San Román de Montoxo, both of which are about 10km away.

Leaving Cuiña, the two routes sync up and proceed westward around the Ría de Santa Marta, following minor roads to the south of AC-862. Pass south around the Ponte de Mera train station, then loop back to the north on DP-6122, leading into

A PONTE DE MERA (9KM)

Bar, pharmacy.

Turn left on AC-862 then right onto DP-6121. Fork right again soon after. 750 meters later, the two routes split; turn left to follow the Mar/Teixido inland. After curving right through a series of small villages, turn left on a dirt track. Rejoin a paved road and proceed into

CASTELO DO CASÓN (4.2KM)

This was a key watchtower in the Middle Ages, although only some stones remain. It offers sweeping views of the Costa Ártabra. The **Fervenza do Casón**, a small waterfall that is easily accessible, follows soon after.

Follow a series of dirt tracks and minor roads for 5.1km, at which point the coastal variant joins from the right. Soon after, depart the paved road at the **Monument to Leslie Howard**. Howard, a British film star and writer in the early 20th century, was active in anti-German propaganda in World War II. His flight was shot down in 1943 by the Luftwaffe, just off the coast. A footpath leads along a spectacular coastal walk into

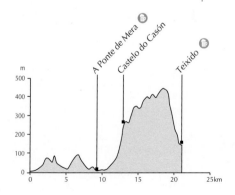

SAN ANDRÉS DE TEIXIDO (7.7KM)

Bars/restaurants. It is possible to taxi into Cedeira for the night and then return to Teixido in the morning: Taxi de Cedeira (tel 673 480 664).

This is one of the most sacred places in Galicia and a major pilgrimage destination. A monastery has existed here since at least the 12th century. The current structure dates to the 16th century, although the marvellous altarpiece is late 18th century. Murals depict the life and martyrdom of Saint Andrew. In the corner, a large number of wax figures have been left representing animals and human bodies – offerings in support of intercession for miraculous healing

Multiple legends exist about Teixido. They share a common beginning: Saint Andrew, or Santo André, apostle and brother of Peter, was stranded by the neighboring cliffs after his boat capsized. After settling here, he grew envious of the pilgrim traffic to Santiago. He complained to God and Saint Peter when they visited; in turn, he was promised that all mortals would come to his sanctuary, living or dead. A variant of the legend notes that those who died without visiting would be reincarnated as lizards, toads, and snakes and then would make the journey.

In the 'Fountain of Three Spouts', pilgrims are advised to drink water from all three pipes, make a wish to Saint Andrew, and throw breadcrumbs into the water. If the crumbs float, the wish will be fulfilled. One of the most common manifestations of faith in Teixido are the Amulets of Saint Andrew, or *sanandresiños*. These are small figures of unfermented bread dough, oven-hardened and painted colourfully, traditionally taking five shapes: hands, fish, rowboats, flowers, and the saint. The festival of Saint Andrew is held on September 8.

The pilgrimage shrine of San Andrés de Teixido

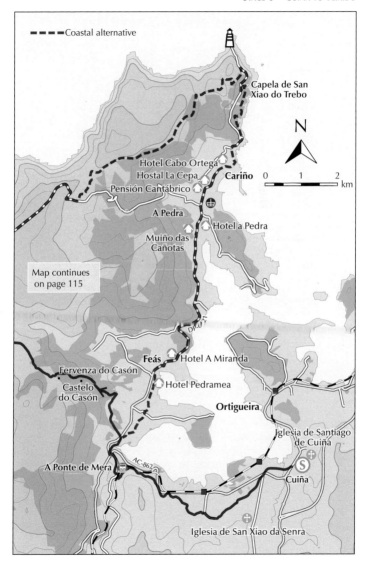

- - - - Coastal alternative

Capela de San
Xiao do Trebo

N

0   1   2
km

Hotel Cabo Ortega
Hostal La Cepa   **Cariño**
Pensión Cantábrico

A Pedra
                      Hotel a Pedra
Muiño das
Cañotas

Map continues
on page 115

DP-01?

Feás Hotel A Miranda

Fervenza do Casón
                      Hotel Pedramea
Castelo
do Casón   **Ortigueira**

                                  Iglesia de Santiago
                                  de Cuiña

A Ponte de Mera   AC-862   Ⓢ
                                   Cuiña
                  Iglesia de San Xiao da Senra

> **Coastal alternative, from Ponte de Mera to Teixido via Cariño**
> Join DP-6121 soon after the route split and continue north to

FEÁS (3.1KM)

Restaurant. **Hotel Pedramea** (doubles €50–55, meals available, @, tel 981 413 008), **Hotel A Miranda** (doubles €90–110, includes breakfast, open Mar–Oct, W/D, @, tel 686 466 814).

> Stick to the DP-6121, continuing to

A PEDRA (5.5KM)

Hotel/Restaurante a Pedra (singles €33, doubles €55, triples €66, laundry, @, tel 981 420 300), **Muiño das Cañotas** (doubles €60–65, open all year, meals available, two-night stay required in summer, tel 698 138 588).

> And again, proceed north on DP-6121 into

CARIÑO (1.9KM)

Bars/restaurants, supermarket. **Pensión Cantábrico** (doubles, meals available, @, tel 981 405 373), **Hostal La Cepa** (doubles €40, meals available, laundry, @, tel 981 405 328), **Hotel Cabo Ortega** (singles €37–52, doubles €48–68, includes breakfast, tel 607 656 700).

The coastline between Cariño and Cedeira features some of the highest cliffs in Europe. Evidence of prehistoric activity in the region is abundant, including flint flakes, castros, and five dolmens in area peaks and caves. While long focused on fisheries, it flourished in the 19th century when Catalan immigrants opened canneries. The local economy was disrupted by labor protests in the late 19th century, generating violent reprisals by the Guardia Civil, and culminating in a surge of unionizing in the early 20th century. After some initial labor successes, Franco's regime came down hard on the region, causing a short-term decline before Cariño rebounded.

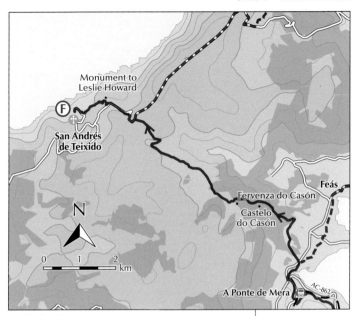

A 16.1km loop around the peninsula follows, passing through entirely rural terrain. An off-road stretch soon after Cariño leads 2.9km to the **Capela de San Xiao do Trebo**, built on an old Roman site and integrating Roman materials into the structure. San Xiao was a fisherman who went hunting one morning; his parents arrived and his wife offered them hospitality, allowing them to rest in her bed. She went to find her husband; he returned on a different trail, discovered a couple in his bed, and killed them. The suffering and repentence that followed ultimately propelled him to sainthood. A Santiago Peregrino statue is inside the chapel.

Cut inland to the highway, passing a restaurant and a roadside fountain, and then continue to the **turnoff for the Cabo Ortegal lighthouse** 1km later. From there, it's all gravel tracks and minor roads until rejoining the Mar 2.6km before **San Andrés de Teixido**.

STAGE 7
Teixido to Xubia

Start	Iglesia de San Andrés de Teixido
Finish	Camino Inglés link in Xubia (alternative Curuxeiras docks, Ferrol)
Distance	36.4km (alternative 79.7km)
% unpaved	33.8%
Total ascent	918m
Total descent	1057m
Terrain	4
Route-finding	3
Accommodation	San Román de Montoxo, O Porto do Cabo, Xubia (alternative route – Cedeira, Valdoviño, Lavacerido, Covas, Vila da Area, Ferrol)

This is a long stage, generally trending downhill, although with a few final ascents along the way. The Mar, which is really the Teixido pilgrim road from Ferrol and recommended here for its relative brevity, proceeds roughly due south through overwhelmingly rural terrain that is interrupted only occasionally by minor villages. Food options are therefore limited. The Mar joins the Inglés in Xubia, at which point those continuing onward will need to decide whether to backtrack to Ferrol or join the Inglés in progress. Alternatively, the coastal approach begins with a gorgeous, well-marked walk on the 'Ruta dos Peiraos' to Cedeira, before following more roads through the next stretch. Yellow arrows appear near Vila da Area and carry onward intermittently to Ferrol. While lovely, this approach covers nearly 80km and thus requires much more time.

Follow a footpath 1.3km south from Teixido. After rejoining a paved road, the two routes split. Turn left on the road to remain on the Mar/Teixido. Waymarks for the 'Camiño Mañon' between Teixido and Xubia are quite good in this stretch. Look for the now-familiar stone balises and white and red arrows painted on the road and on signs. Fork right off the road soon after onto a dirt track, before rejoining a

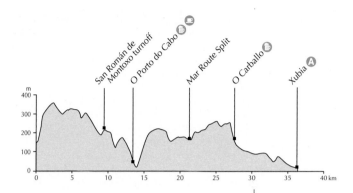

paved road leading into **Reboredo**, 2.1km later (fountain).
A similar mix of paved and dirt tracks continues as you
proceed southward, crossing AC-566 at the

SAN ROMÁN DE MONTOXO TURNOFF (8.9KM)

The village of San Román is off-route to the east, with two possible accommodation options. Follow the unmarked route 900 meters to **Casa a Pasada** (doubles €50–00, includes breakfast, tel 659 330 892) or 1.4km to **Casa as Jarras** (doubles €58–70, includes breakfast, dinner possible with advance notice, tel 618 665 218)

The **Igrexa de San Román de Montoxo** is a modern edifice.

   The route moves onward in a southwest direction,
passing through the village of **Sisalde** 2km later, and then
continuing on to

O PORTO DO CABO (4.9KM)

Bar. **Casa do Morcego** (doubles €60–89, includes breakfast, dinner available, W/D, @, tel 981 483 282).

The village is built around the medieval bridge over the Río das Mestas, formerly a key link in the royal road between Ferrol and Cedeira. The **Casa da Bastona** is a 16th-century structure near the bridge that once provided accommodation to pilgrims.

117

After crossing AC-102 and the Río das Mestas into town, turn left and follow a series of minor roads and tracks 4km, roughly due west toward the **Ermida de Liñeiro** and its highly acclaimed Renaissance altarpiece. Also known as the Capela da Fame, it was actually moved to this spot in its entirety by the parish priest. When pilgrims started following a different route to Teixido at that time, bypassing the shrine, the Virgin expressed her desire that he relocate it through a series of signs. Continue westward for 1.4km to the **Embalse das Forcadas** (the Igrexa de San Pedro de Loira, with its late-Gothic dome, is 1.3km south on CP-2502 – turn left immediately after the dam to reach it) and 1.4km more to the **Antiga Igrexa de San Pedro turnoff**. Soon after the road curves south, arrive at the

MAR ROUTE SPLIT (8.2KM)

Both branches of the Mar pass through heavily-forested hills with little contact with villages and no facilities. Similarly, they both ultimately pass through Carballo, although they don't overlap. Most facilities are closer to the western approach which we recommend – stay on the road at the route split for this option. Add 1.3km if you take the eastern approach.

O CARBALLO (5.9KM)

Restaurants.

The recommended western approach is once again through wooded terrain, swinging wide to the southwest, and brushing against the edge of **Carreira de Arriba** (Casa Veiga – doubles €42, includes breakfast, @, tel 981 485 341) 3km later before heading more fully southward to rejoin the eastern route prior to Sequeiros. The eastern approach is largely highway-bound through a more exposed valley, passing through a series of small villages.

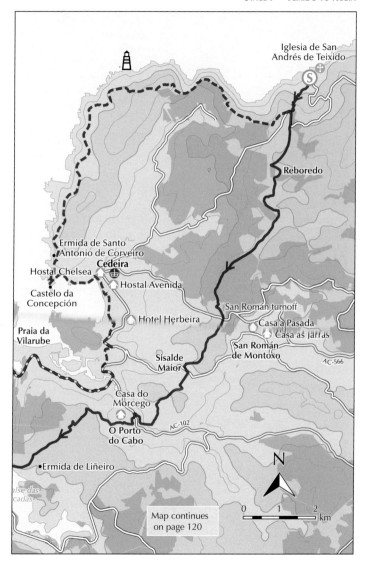

Map continues
on page 120

119

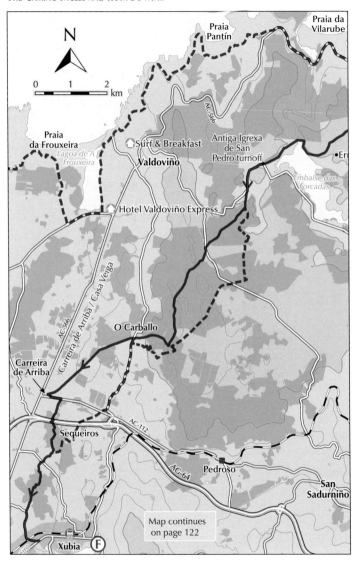

Map continues on page 122

This route is 600 meters shorter than the western approach. From **Sequeiros** the two routes are unified for the final approach, leading southward to the Molino de las Aceñas, one of Galicia's major flour factories in the 19th century.

XUBIA (8.5KM)

See the Camino Inglés, Stage 1, for facilities information.

From here, pilgrims have several options. It's possible to turn left, join the Camino Inglés, and carry on to Santiago. Alternatively, one could turn right and back-track along the Inglés, to the **Mosteiro do Couto**, where many pilgrims historically began their walk to Teixido, as documented in Padre Sarmiento's account from 1755, or continue all the way to Ferrol. It's also possible to catch the train from the nearby station.

The last/first waymark for the Teixido pilgrimage in Xubia

Coastal alternative, from Teixido to Ferrol

Waymarks are limited throughout the coastal approach, although you will find some white and yellow arrows painted on the road at key intersections on the initial stretch to Cedeira, including the initial route split. Known as the 'Ruta dos Peiraos,' this is a fantastic walk, almost entirely off-road with consistently excellent views. Be prepared – it is quite strenuous.

CEDEIRA (16.3KM)

All facilities. **Hotel Herbeira** (singles €60–105, doubles €70–125, triples €95–145, quads €115–160, closed Dec–Jan holidays, meals available, laundry, @), **Hostal Chelsea** (doubles €35–42, Plaza Sagrado Corazón 10, tel 981 482 340), **Hostal Avenida** (doubles, meals available, @, tel 981 492 112).

A long-inhabited area, as reflected in the pre-Roman settlement of Serra da Capelada, some 4000 years old. Cedeira was first documented in the 11th century, but it reached a peak in the 13th century with town walls and a thriving port.

The **Castillo de la Concepción** (Tue–Sat 1030–2000, Sun 1200–1400, 1600–2000), built at the mouth of the port, west of Cedeira, was established in the 19th century to protect the city from attacks by the English. The **Ruta das Portas** is a scenic walk through town that visits each of the four surviving town gates.

The **O Museo Mares** (mid-Jul to mid-Sep, Tue–Sun 1030–1330, 1730–1930, weekends only rest of year) tells the history of Cedeiran seafaring, displaying traditional boats and fishing gear, fossils, and shells.

Proceed almost due south from Cedeira, following a series of minor roads until joining AC-566 just prior to the Río das Mestas. Cross the river and follow the highway to

PRAIA DE VILARUBE (6.3KM)

Bar.

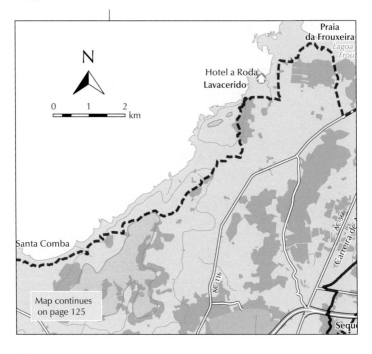

Map continues on page 125

The stunning beach of Praia de Pantín, following the coastal variant

Continue along AC-566 for 2.5km, then fork right onto a minor road, leading to the

PRAIA DE PANTÍN (4KM)

Bar/restaurant.

This beach, like many in the area, is very popular with surfers. It hosts the Pantín Classic, a qualifying event for the World Surf League each August/September.

Follow a pedestrian track around the beach and then join a minor road leading around the neighboring peninsula and through the next section of the coast. Skirt the edge of

VALDOVIÑO (6.7KM)

Bars/restaurants, supermarket, mostly located off-route in town center. **Surf & Breakfast** (€25–28.50, includes breakfast, kitchen, @, Avda Ferrol), **Hotel Valdoviño Express** (doubles €45–50, includes breakfast, @, tel 629 888 008) has a wonderfully informative website, with good information on the Teixido route.

Like much of the region, prehistoric settlements are sprinkled throughout the greater Valdoviño area. Romans moved into the region in the first to the fourth centuries, pursuing gold, silver, and tin. Christianity spread widely throughout the area in the centuries that followed, with many extant churches established in the 12th century. The road to San Andrés brought travelers, money, and greater social organization, as towns such as Valdoviño began to coalesce. In the modern era, Valdoviño's city council declared the Republic in 1931, the first such council to do so. During the Franco years, small-scale rebellions against government appointees took place on multiple occasions. Street lights came in 1942, a police station in 1965, and sidewalks a year later.

> Follow the coastal road out of town. Soon after, it becomes a pedestrian track. Turn right on AC-116 and then right again at the next roundabout, proceeding directly to the **Praia da Frouxeira**. Cross the beach, continuing west until arriving at the coast once more, and then join a road southward. At the next intersection, turn right and pass the edge of

LAVACERIDO (8.5KM)

Bars/restaurants. **Hotel a Roda** (doubles €50–55, triples/quads, @, tel 981 486 263).

> Fork right onto an off-road stretch, known as the 'Senda Litoral Costa Artabra' and leading through a series of old military defences and then climbing to the Coto das Penas and then the Montes de Lagoa. Finally, join DP-3606 as it leads to

PRAIA DA FRAGATA (14.5KM)

Situated in the midst of a long stretch of three straight beaches, preceded by Praia de Vilar and followed by Praia de Esmelle. **Camping As Cabazas** has a bar and grocery.

> Join Praia de Esmelle, crossing both it and Praia de San Xurxo before proceeding inland to the entrance to

VILA DA AREA (2.7KM)

Restaurant. **The Camp Doñinos** (€30, tel 605 182 537) offers dorm beds with lots of amenities, including surfboards.

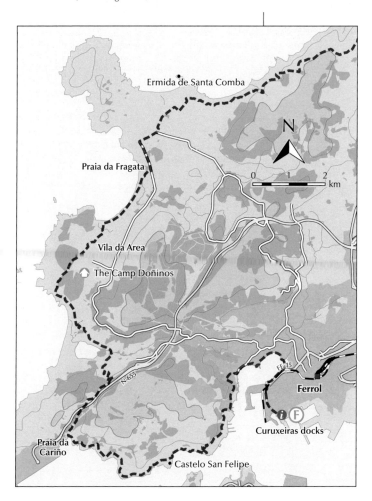

Proceed back to the coast, following one more beachfront walk before climbing inland. Follow a series of minor roads southeast, turning right just before reaching N-655 and then crossing it shortly before arriving in

PRAIA CARIÑO (8.3KM)

Praia Cariño is situated at the mouth of the Ría de Ferrol, unfortunately close to the outer port of Ferrol and its industrial byproducts. Evidence of Ferrol's old network of fortifications is apparent here, although it increases markedly as you approach the city. It is believed that the largest ship in the Spanish Armada, the *Ragazzona*, sank here in 1588.

A waterfront track leads east, passing the aforementioned fortifications, including their linchpin – the Castelo de San Felipe. Loop around Ferrol's naval base before arriving in the city center.

FERROL (12.4KM)

See the Camino Inglés, Stage 1, for facilities information.

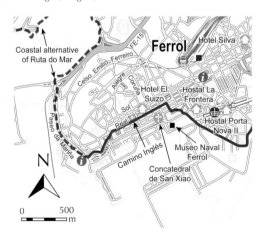

THE CAMINO FINISTERRE

The final approach toward the coast (Finisterre, Stage 3)

INTRODUCTION

For many modern pilgrims, the walk does not end in Santiago de Compostela. Instead, they are drawn still farther west, as far as the land will permit. They walk to Finisterre, the 'end of the world.'

During Roman times, Finisterre was believed to be the westernmost point in Europe – and therefore the end of the world. (It turns out that Portugal's Cabo da Roca is farther west, and there is more to the world beyond Europe.) While there is no firm evidence about when the pilgrimage to Finisterre began, its perceived geographic position accorded it a certain status that would have carried special meaning for a pagan population. The Christian trek thus ends on a pagan track. Many of today's pilgrims tap into their own primal instincts, burning their clothes at the lighthouse while watching the sunset. We do not recommend this; wildfires have been started in the process.

The pilgrimage to Finisterre can be completed comfortably in three days, but the emergence of new private albergues over the last few years makes it easy to take a more leisurely pace. As was the case on the camino, pilgrims should get sellos every day (ideally two per day); upon arrival in Finisterre, it is possible to get a certificate (the Fisterrana), similar to the Compostela. The route is very well marked, the only potential complication being that it is marked in both directions allowing pilgrims to make the return trip. And, while Finisterre may be the 'end of the world', it doesn't have to be the end of your pilgrimage, as an additional walk to Muxía and another traditional pilgrim shrine is possible and increasingly popular. Located north of Finisterre, this can be reached via waymarked routes from Finisterre and Hospital.

STAGE 1

Santiago de Compostela to Negreira

Start	Praza do Obradoiro, Santiago de Compostela
Finish	Albergue El Carmen, Negreira
Distance	20.5km
% unpaved	30%
Total ascent	501m
Total descent	592m
Terrain	4
Route-finding	1
Pilgrim accommodation	Castelo, Negreira

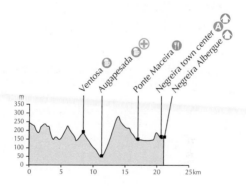

With your back to Santiago cathedral, proceed down the steps out of the back-right corner of the **Praza do Obradoiro**. Keep straight on through several intersections until arriving in the Carballeira de San Lourenzo, a small park. Turn right through the park and then left down a minor cement road. Proceed through modest **Piñeiro**, the tiny village of Villestro and cross the Río Roxos, leading into

VENTOSA (8.7KM)

Bar, with excellent food options.

Follow a mix of minor roads and AC-453 through Lombao. Turn here for **Albergue Casa Riamonte** (€12, 8 beds, W/D, tel 981 890 356, located in Castelo 500 meters off-route). As you approach a T-junction, turn left past a medieval bridge into

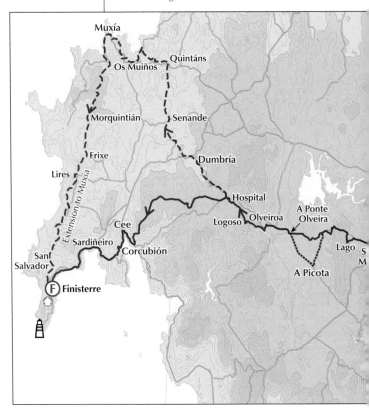

AUGAPESADA (2.8KM)

Bar with small grocery, pharmacy.

Proceed along a mix of dirt tracks and paved roads, including a surprisingly sharp ascent. Pass through Carballo and Trasmonte (bar), continuing to

PONTE MACEIRA (5.2KM)

Bar/restaurant.

This may be the prettiest town on the whole camino. The medieval bridge over the Río Tambre overlooks boulders on one side and a fortress-like pazo on the other. The river is dammed, and a rope swing on the northwest side has tempted even the most determined of walkers into a lengthy break.

Cross the bridge and turn left. Follow a series of well-marked minor roads, winding back and forth across AC-544. Continue through Barca, soon passing Albergue Anjana (€12, 18 beds, W/D, tel 607 387 229) on the way into

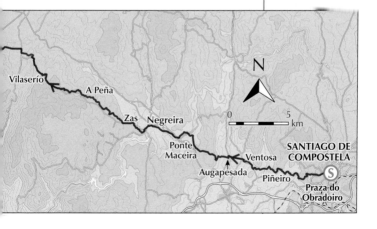

NEGREIRA (3.8KM)

This busy little town with all facilities presents your best opportunity to stock up before reaching the coast. **Albergue de Peregrinos** on the way out of town (€6, 20 beds, kitchen, @, tel 664 081 498) and four private albergues: **Lua** (€12, 40 beds, kitchen, W/D, @, Avda de Santiago 22, tel 698 128 883), **San José** (€12, 50 beds, kitchen, W/D, @, Rúa de Castelao 20, tel 881 976 934), **El Carmen** (€12, 24 beds, meals, W/D, @, c/del Carmen, tel 981 881 652), **Alecrin** (€12, 42 beds, open Apr–Nov, kitchen, W/D, @, Avda Santiago 52, tel 981 818 286). **Hostal La Mezquita** (singles €30, doubles €50, c/del Carmen 2, tel 636 129 691).

STAGE 2
Negreira to Olveiroa

Start	Albergue El Carmen, Negreira
Finish	Albergue de Peregrinos, Olveiroa
Distance	34.1km
% unpaved	37%
Total ascent	601m
Total descent	492m
Terrain	2
Route-finding	1
Pilgrim accommodation	A Peña, Vilaserío, Santa Mariña, Lago, A Ponte Olveira, Olveiroa

Follow the arrows back to the camino, soon ascending a tree-covered footpath. Re-emerge on AC-5603 and proceed into

ZAS (3.3KM)

Bar with small grocery along left side of highway (poorly marked).

Fork right off the highway. A combination of footpaths and dirt tracks follows, leading through Rapote and onward to

A PEÑA (5.1KM)

Bars, grocery, **Albergue Alto da Pena** (€12, 20 beds, meals, W/D, tel 609 853 486).

Rejoin the highway before diverging once again onto dirt tracks. Follow AC-5603 to

VILASERÍO (5.4KM)

Bar. **Albergue de Peregrinos** on the road out of town (€6, sleeping pads on floor, tel 648 792 029), **Albergue Casa Vella** (€12, 12 beds, singles €25+, doubles €35+, kitchen, meals available, W, tel 981 893 516), **Albergue O Rueiro** (€12, open Mar–Oct, 30 beds, W/D, tel 981 893 561).

Follow the highway out of town, then turn right to pass through Cornado. Continue on a series of dirt tracks and minor roads into Maroñas, before joining AC-400 into

SANTA MARIÑA (8.1KM)

Bars. **Albergue Santa Mariña** (€10, 21 beds, meals available, W/D, tel 981 852 097), **Albergue Casa Pepa** (€12, 18 beds, meals available, W/D, tel 981 852 881).

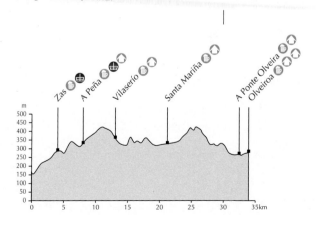

133

Waymark on the way to Vilaserío

Continue through the small towns of Gueima, Vilar de Castro, and Lago (**Albergue Monto Oro** – €12, 28 beds, open Mar–Nov, W/D, @, tel 682 586 157).

A Picota variant

Those seeking more facilities today should consider this route. About 1km on from Lago, at a minor intersection with a bus shelter and signs for Casa Jurjo and Abeleiroas, ignore the waymarks and keep straight on. Follow the road for 3km, then turn right at the T-junction into the center of A Picota, which offers all facilities, including **Albergue Picota** (€15, 6 beds, doubles €35, W/D, tel 981 852 019) and the pilgrim-friendly **Casa Jurjo** (singles €30–35, doubles €45–60, pilgrim discounts, tel 981 852 015). At the main intersection in town, turn right on AC-3404, rejoining the official route in Mallón and continuing into A Ponte Olveira. This detour is 6.8km, making it 3km longer than the official route.

Staying primarily on minor roads, pass the church of **San Cristovo de Corzón** and continue onto AC-3404 in **Mallón**. Cross the Río Xallas to arrive in

A PONTE OLVEIRA (10.4KM)

Bar/restaurant. **Albergue-Pensión Ponte Olveira** (€12 beds, 20 beds, doubles €30, open Easter–Oct, kitchen, W/D, @, tel 603 450 145).

Continue on AC-3404. Fork left off the highway into

OLVEIROA (1.8KM)

Bars/restaurants. **Albergue de Peregrinos** (€6, 34 beds, kitchen, tel 981 744 001), **Albergue Hórreo** (€12, 53 beds, kitchen, W/D, @, tel 981 741 673), **Albergue O Peregrino** (€12, 12 beds, W/D, meals available, tel 981 741 682), **Casa Loncho** (doubles €40, triples €60, tel 981 741 673), **Casa Rural As Pias** (singles €40, doubles €50–60, tel 981 741 520).

The camino has transformed no town more over the last decade than Olveiroa. When the authors first visited it in 2004, it was covered in a thick layer of cow manure, had one bar offering little food, and was in a general state of disrepair. Today, flowerbeds line the camino, new bars and accommodations seem to pop up daily, and traditional buildings are being restored.

STAGE 3
Olveiroa to Finisterre

Start	Albergue de Peregrinos, Olveiroa
Finish	Albergue de Peregrinos, Finisterre
Distance	32.2km
% unpaved	66%
Total ascent	468m
Total descent	728m
Terrain	3
Route-finding	2
Pilgrim accommodation	Logoso, Hospital, Cee, Corcubión, Finisterre

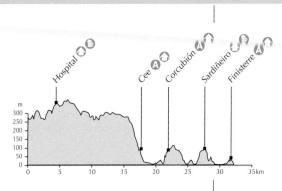

Continue straight through town, soon forking left off-road. Follow the route as it dips and climbs through **Logoso** (Albergue O Logoso – €12, 22 beds, singles €35, kitchen, W/D, tel 659 505 399). Continue into

135

HOSPITAL (4.9KM)

Bar offering excellent bocadillos and the last opportunity for food or water until the coast. Refill water here. **Albergue O Casteliño** (€12, 18 beds, private room, meals available, W/D, tel 615 997 169).

For details of the Muxía option, see Extension to Muxía, below.

The camino splits 600 meters after the bar at a highway roundabout. Pilgrims continuing to Finisterre turn left, while those heading for Muxía should turn right. ◄

Follow the road, then fork right onto a gravel track. From here to Cee the route is entirely off-road, completely rural, and offers sweeping views. Along the way, pass by 15th-century Santuario de Nosa Señora das Neves. There is a sacred fountain here, and a local pilgrimage to the site every year. In another 3km, arrive at Ermita de San Pedro Mártir, which has a sacred fountain of its own. The descent to Cee begins soon after, with views of the coast, including Cabo Finisterre, unfolding beneath.

Head downhill, reaching the *cruceiro* (crucifix) next to the Igrexa de Nosa Señora da Xunqueira in the center of

CEE (14.1KM)

Modern beach town with all facilities and many private albergues, including **O Bordón** (€12, 24 beds, kitchen, tel 981 746 574), **Casa da Fonte** (€11, 42 beds, Rúa de Arriba 36, tel 699 242 711), **Moreira** (€12, 22 beds, open late-Apr–early-Nov, kitchen, W/D, c/Rosalía de Castro, tel 620 891 547) and **Tequerón** (€12–15, 8 beds, W/D, @, Rúa de Arriba 31, tel 666 119 594). **Hotel Insua** (singles €45–55, doubles €50–65, Avda Finisterre 82, tel 981 747 575), **Hotel La Marina** (singles €35–45, doubles €50–65, Avda Fernando Blanco 26, tel 981 747 381).

Proceed through the center of town, eventually forking right uphill to reach

CORCUBIÓN (2.4KM)

All facilities. **Albergue de Peregrinos San Roque** on outskirts of town (donativo,

16 beds, communal meals, tel 679 460 942), **Albergue Camiño de Fisterra** (€10, Avda Fisterra 220, tel 981 745 040). Many hotels, including: **Casa da Balea** (singles €40+, doubles €50+, c/Rafael Juan 44, tel 981 746 645), **Casa Bernarda** (singles €35+, doubles €70+, Plaza Párroco Francisco Sánchez 3, tel 981 747 157).

Proceed left uphill out of the plaza. At the 13th-century Iglesia San Marcos, turn right upstairs and then curve right, proceeding along a footpath between high walls. Climb past the Albergue de Peregrinos. At the Encrucijada de San Roque, veer right onto a footpath, before returning to the highway in Amarela. Follow the route on a series of small roads and tracks through Estorde (**bars, grocery in campsite; Hostal Playa de Estorde** – singles €40–50, doubles €60–80, tel 981 745 585). Keep straight on AC-445 into

SARDIÑEIRO (4.7KM)

Bars, restaurants. **Hotel Merendero** (singles €20, doubles €35, tel 981 743 535), **Pensión Playa de Sardiñeiro** (doubles €40, triples €60, tel 981 743 741).

From here, the route winds around and occasionally joins AC-445, before eventually forking left onto the Corredoira de Don Camilo and descending to the Praia de Langosteira. Once there, you can follow the paved walkway or remove your shoes and splash along the beach. At the beach's end, return to AC-445. Fork left on Avda de A Coruña and proceed into

FINISTERRE (6.1KM)

All facilities. **Albergue de Peregrinos** (€6, 36 beds, kitchen, W/D, c/Real 2, tel 981 740 781). Many private albergues, including **Finistellae** (€12, 20 beds, kitchen, W/D, @, c/Manuel Lago Pais 7, tel 637 821 296), **Sol e da Lúa** (€11, 18 beds, private rooms, kitchen, W/D, @, c/Atalaya 7, tel 881 108 710), **Cabo da Vila** (€12, 28 beds, private rooms, kitchen, W/D, @, Avda da Coruña 13, tel 607 735 474) and **Paz** (€12–15, 30 beds, W/D, @, c/Victor Cardalda 11, tel 981 740 332). **Hostal**

The 'end of the world' at Finisterre

Mariquito (singles €25–30, doubles €36–48, c/Santa Catalina 44, tel 981 740 044), **Hotel A Langosteira** (singles €32–42, doubles €40–52, Avda de Coruña 61, tel 981 740 543), **Hotel Áncora** (singles €28+, doubles €35+, c/Alcalde Fernández 43, tel 981 740 791). The certificate commemorating your pilgrimage to Finisterre, the Fisterrana, is available from the municipal Albergue de Peregrinos.

Buses returning to Santiago depart from the stop situated around the corner from the municipal albergue. The service is run by Monbus, with eight departures on weekdays (the first leaves at 0820, the last at 1900), six on Saturdays, and five on Sundays/holidays. The earliest departure on weekends is 0945. The trip takes up to three hours and costs €9.85. Schedules can change, so double-check with Monbus in advance: www.monbus.es.

Although you have arrived in the town of Finisterre, the **lighthouse** at the 'end of the world' remains 3.3km away, following AC-4408. Heading there after an early dinner is recommended, as this gives you a few hours of daylight to climb around the point and enjoy the views before watching the sunset. Bring a flashlight for the walk home. Most albergues allow pilgrims to return late, but double-check in advance. It is now possible to sleep next to the lighthouse in the Hotel O Semáforo (doubles €99–150, tel 981 110 210).

Extension to Muxía
Many pilgrims, not ready to go home, add Muxía to their itinerary – either before or after they visit Finisterre. Medieval pilgrims are documented as having made

the trek to Muxía to visit the Santuario de la Virgen de la Barca, although the current structure dates to 1719. Located on the coast north of Finisterre, Muxía can be reached via waymarked routes from both Olveiroa and Finisterre.

Those visiting Muxía before Finisterre will fork right when the camino splits shortly after **Hospital** (see Camino Finisterre, Stage 3), 6km after Olveiroa. From there, the route covers 25.5km. The best place for supplies along the way is **Dumbría**, 4.6km from the fork (**bars, grocery store**, and **Albergue de Peregrinos** – €6, 26 beds, kitchen, tel 981 744 001). Bars are also available in **Senande** (5.5km), **Quintáns** (5.2km), and **Os Muiños** (5.6km), with several others sprinkled over the remaining 4.5km to **Muxía**.

The route between Finisterre and Muxía spans 27km of rugged Galician countryside. Plan ahead. The only facilities available on this route are in **Lires**, which is nearly halfway between the two towns (two **bars** and several places to stay: **Casa Raúl** – doubles €30–58, tel 981 748 156, and **Albergue As Eiras** – €12, 22 beds, W/D, tel 981 748 180). It is critical to get your credenciál stamped in Lires if you hope to either obtain a certificate or stay in the municipal albergues. For more information on the route, including detailed turn-by-turn directions, visit the Confraternity of Saint James website (www.csj.org.uk), where an online guide is available.

MUXÍA

Muxía has all facilities, including an **Albergue de Peregrinos** (€6, 32 beds, kitchen, c/Enfesto 22, tel 610 264 325) and many private albergues including: **Albergue@Muxia** (€11, 40 beds, kitchen, W/D, @, c/Enfesto 12, tel 651 627 768), **Bela Muxia** (€12, 52 beds, private rooms, kitchen, W/D, @, Rúa Encarnación 30, tel 687 798 222) and **da Costa** (€10, 10 beds, kitchen, W/D, Avda Doctor Toba 33, tel 676 363 820). As was true in Finisterre, there is a certificate given to those who walk this route, available from the municipal albergue. There are two direct buses per day from Muxía to Santiago. As before, for more information on the route, visit www.csj.org.uk and refer to the online guide.

Santuario de la Virgen de la Barca in Muxía

APPENDIX A

Useful sources of information

Updated information on albergues

Eroski/Consumer Camino de Santiago is the best resource online for up-to-date albergue information, on all of the major caminos.
caminodesantiago.consumer.es

Gronze is another excellent resource.
www.gronze.com

Transport

For additional information see 'Getting there and back' in the Introduction.

Bus
Movelia: www.movelia.es

ALSA: www.alsa.es

Monbus: www.monbus.es

Empresa Freire:
www.empresafreire.com

Arriva: www.arriva.gal

Train
Renfe: www.renfe.com

Air
RyanAir: www.ryanair.com

EasyJet: www.easyjet.com

Vueling: www.vueling.com

Iberia: www.iberia.com

Air Europa: www.aireuropa.com

Air Berlin: www.airberlin.com

Baggage transport

On the Camino Inglés contact correos:
www.elcaminoconcorreos.com/es/.
Your only likely option on the Ruta do Mar is to coordinate with your accommodation and a local taxi to move your pack ahead, although this will cost much more.

Credenciál

Before departure, you can obtain the credenciál from Camino-related groups including:

Confraternity of Saint James (CSJ):
www.csj.org.uk

American Pilgrims:
www.americanpilgrims.com

Canadian Company of Pilgrims:
www.santiago.ca

Camino Society Ireland:
www.caminosociety.com

Once you arrive in Spain, the credenciál can be obtained from the tourist office in Ribadeo, the concatedral and turismos in Ferrol, and the pilgrim office in Santiago de Compostela. Always confirm availability in advance, via email.

APPENDIX B

English–Spanish–Gallego glossary

English	Spanish	Gallego
altarpiece	retablo	retablo
bakery	panadería	panadería
bathroom	baño/aseo/servicio	baño
beach	playa	praia
beware of dog	cuidado con el perro	coidado co can
bill (in a restaurant)	cuenta	factura
blister	ampolla	bocha
bridge	puente	ponte
building	edificio	edificio
bull ring	plaza de toros	praza de touros
bus station	estación de autobuses	estación de autobuses
butcher's shop	carnicería	carnicería
central plaza	plaza mayor	praza maior
chapel	capilla	capela
church	iglesia	igrexa
city	ciudad	cidade
close the gate	cierren la puerta	pechen a porta
closed	cerrado	pechado
clothes washing place	lavadero	lavadoiro
corn crib/granary	hórreo	hórreo
corner	esquina	esquina
crucifix	cruceiro	cruceiro
dam	embalse	embalse
detour	desvío	desvío
doctor	médico, doctor	médico, doutor
donation	donativo	donativo
door, gate	puerta	porta
far	lejos	lonxe

English	Spanish	Gallego
food	*comida*	*comida*
fountain	*fuente*	*fonte*
goodbye	*adiós*	*adeus*
good morning	*buenos días*	*bos días*
guesthouse	*casa de huéspedes*	*casa de hóspedes*
help	*ayuda, socorro*	*axuda, socorro*
here	*aquí*	*aquí*
hermitage	*ermita*	*ermida*
highway	*carretera*	*estrada*
hill	*colina*	*cerro*
historic center	*casco antiguo*	*casco antigo*
hospital	*hospital*	*hospital*
hotel	*hotel, hostal*	*hotel, hostal*
how much is it?	*cuanto cuesta?*	*canto costa?*
hunting preserve	*coto de caza*	*coto de caza*
inn	*fonda, hospedaje*	*fonda, hospedaxe*
kiosk (tobacco)	*estanco, tabac*	*estanco, tabac*
left	*izquierda*	*esquerda*
manor house	*pazo*	*pazo*
mill	*molino*	*muíño*
monastery	*monasterio*	*mosteiro*
near	*cerca*	*preto*
neighborhood	*barrio*	*barrio*
no	*no*	*non*
open	*abierto*	*aberto*
pain	*dolor*	*dor*
path	*camino, senda*	*camiño, senda*
petrol station	*gasolinera*	*gasolineira*

English	Spanish	Gallego
pilgrim	peregrino	peregrino
pilgrim hostel	albergue de peregrinos	albergue de peregrinos
please	por favor	por favor
post office	correos	correos
prehistoric fort	castro	castro
restaurant	restaurante	restaurante
right	derecha	dereita
roadside cross	cruce de carretera	cruzamento de estrada
sports center	polideportivo	polideportivo
Saint James	santiago	santiago
stamp	sello	selo
stepping stones	peldaños	banzos
straight	recto, directamente	dereito
stream	arroyo	arroio
street	calle	rúa
supermarket	supermercado	supermercado
telephone	teléfono	teléfono
time	hora	hora
thank you	gracias	grazas
tourist office	turismo	turismo
town	pueblo	pobo
town hall	ayuntamiento	concello
valley	valle	val
view point	mirador	miradoiro
water (drinkable)	agua potable	auga potable
waymark	señal	sinal
where	donde	onde
yes	sí	si
youth hostel	albergue juveníl	albergue xuvenil

APPENDIX C
Suggestions for further reading

Although an overwhelming amount of literature has been produced about the Camino Francés, very little is available in English on the Camino Inglés and next-to-nothing on the Ruta do Mar.

Friends of the Camino de Santiago websites

Asociación Galega de Amigos: Includes route descriptions and albergue information for all of the Caminos de Santiago through Galicia, but not the Mar. www.amigosdelcamino.com

Asociación de Amigos del Camino de Santiago de Lugo: Includes route maps for both the Inglés and Mar. www.lugocamino.com

The Confraternity of Saint James: Based in London, this continues to be the pre-eminent source for English-language information on the Caminos de Santiago. www.csj.org.uk

Other recommended guides

Johnnie Walker, *Camino de Santiago Pilgrim Guides: Camino Inglés*, London: CSJ, 2018. Those seeking detailed turn-by-turn instructions for the Inglés should pick up this affordable guide, available in print and ebook editions. Walker is a major advocate for the Inglés and his work – and the CSJ's – is worth supporting.

Xoán Ramón Fernández Pacios, *Camiño do Mar*, Deputación de Lugo. This is the best available guide to the Mar, although it is in Gallego. www.calameo.com/books/00066802104fd63f2c828

The Camino Forum has outstanding, on-the-ground posts from pilgrims on the Mar and Inglés. www.caminodesantiago.me/community

Books on pilgrimage, Santiago, and Galicia

Several pilgrim journals on the Camino Inglés experience have been published in recent years, including Susan Jagannath's *The Camino Inglés: 6 days (or less) to Santiago*, and Jeffrey Zurschmeide's *The Camino Less Traveled By: A Photographic Pilgrimage*.

Jonathan Sumption, *The Age of Pilgrimage: The Medieval Journey to God*, Mahwah: HiddenSpring, 2003. A detailed survey of the pilgrimage boom in the medieval Christian world.

Phil Cousineau, *The Art of Pilgrimage*, San Francisco: Canari Press, 2012. A multi-faceted look at pilgrimage and the pilgrim experience.

Sharif Gemie, *Galicia (Histories of Europe)*, Cardiff: University of Wales Press, 2006. The best concise history of the region of Galicia.

DOWNLOAD THE ROUTES
IN GPX FORMAT

All the routes in this guide are available for download from:

www.cicerone.co.uk/1006/GPX

as GPX files. You should be able to load them into most formats of mobile device, whether GPS or smartphone.

When you go to this link, you will be asked for your email address and where you purchased the guide, and have the option to subscribe to the Cicerone e-newsletter.

www.cicerone.co.uk

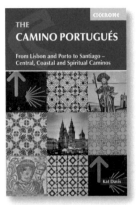
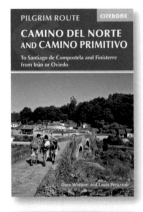

LISTING OF CICERONE GUIDES

SCOTLAND

Backpacker's Britain:
  Northern Scotland
Ben Nevis and Glen Coe
Cycling in the Hebrides
Great Mountain Days in Scotland
Mountain Biking in Southern and
  Central Scotland
Mountain Biking in West and
  North West Scotland
Not the West Highland Way
  Scotland
Scotland's Best Small Mountains
Scotland's Mountain Ridges
Scrambles in Lochaber
The Ayrshire and Arran Coastal
  Paths
The Border Country
The Borders Abbeys Way
The Cape Wrath Trail
The Great Glen Way
The Great Glen Way Map Booklet
The Hebridean Way
The Hebrides
The Isle of Mull
The Isle of Skye
The Skye Trail
The Southern Upland Way
The Speyside Way
The Speyside Way Map Booklet
The West Highland Way
Walking Highland Perthshire
Walking in Scotland's Far North
Walking in the Angus Glens
Walking in the Cairngorms
Walking in the Ochils, Campsie
  Fells and Lomond Hills
Walking in the Pentland Hills
Walking in the Southern Uplands
Walking in Torridon
Walking Loch Lomond and the
  Trossachs
Walking on Arran
Walking on Harris and Lewis
Walking on Rum and the Small
  Isles
Walking on the Orkney and
  Shetland Isles
Walking on Uist and Barra
Walking the Corbetts Vol 1 South
  of the Great Glen
Walking the Corbetts Vol 2 North
  of the Great Glen
Walking the Munros
  Vol 1 – Southern, Central and
  Western Highlands
Walking the Munros
  Vol 2 – Northern Highlands
  and the Cairngorms

West Highland Way Map Booklet
Winter Climbs Ben Nevis and
  Glen Coe
Winter Climbs in the Cairngorms

NORTHERN ENGLAND TRAILS

Hadrian's Wall Path
Hadrian's Wall Path Map Booklet
Pennine Way Map Booklet
The Coast to Coast Map Booklet
The Coast to Coast Walk
The Dales Way
The Dales Way Map Booklet
The Pennine Way

LAKE DISTRICT

Cycling in the Lake District
Great Mountain Days in the Lake
  District
Lake District Winter Climbs
Lake District: High Level and
  Fell Walks
Lake District: Low Level and
  Lake Walks
Mountain Biking in the Lake
  District
Outdoor Adventures with
  Children – Lake District
Scrambles in the Lake District
  – North
Scrambles in the Lake District
  – South
Short Walks in Lakeland
  Book 1: South Lakeland
Short Walks in Lakeland
  Book 2: North Lakeland
Short Walks in Lakeland
  Book 3: West Lakeland
The Cumbria Way
Tour of the Lake District
Trail and Fell Running in the Lake
  District

NORTH WEST ENGLAND
AND THE ISLE OF MAN

Cycling the Pennine Bridleway
Cycling the Way of the Roses
Isle of Man Coastal Path
The Lancashire Cycleway
The Lune Valley and Howgills
The Ribble Way
Walking in Cumbria's Eden Valley
Walking in Lancashire
Walking in the Forest of Bowland
  and Pendle
Walking on the Isle of Man
Walking on the West Pennine
  Moors
Walks in Ribble Country
Walks in Silverdale and Arnside

NORTH EAST ENGLAND,
YORKSHIRE DALES
AND PENNINES

Cycling in the Yorkshire Dales
Great Mountain Days in the
  Pennines
Mountain Biking in the Yorkshire
  Dales
South Pennine Walks
St Oswald's Way and
  St Cuthbert's Way
The Cleveland Way and the
  Yorkshire Wolds Way
The Cleveland Way Map Booklet
The North York Moors
The Reivers Way
The Teesdale Way
Trail and Fell Running in the
  Yorkshire Dales
Walking in County Durham
Walking in Northumberland
Walking in the North Pennines
Walking in the Yorkshire Dales:
  North and East
Walking in the Yorkshire Dales:
  South and West
Walks in Dales Country
Walks in the Yorkshire Dales

WALES AND WELSH BORDERS

Cycling Lôn Las Cymru
Glyndwr's Way
Great Mountain Days in
  Snowdonia
Hillwalking in Shropshire
Hillwalking in Wales – Vol 1
Hillwalking in Wales – Vol 2
Mountain Walking in Snowdonia
Offa's Dyke Map Booklet
Offa's Dyke Path
Ridges of Snowdonia
Scrambles in Snowdonia
The Ascent of Snowdon
The Ceredigion and Snowdonia
  Coast Paths
The Pembrokeshire Coast Path
Pembrokeshire Coast Path Map
  Booklet
The Severn Way
The Snowdonia Way
The Wales Coast Path
The Wye Valley Walk
Walking in Carmarthenshire
Walking in Pembrokeshire
Walking in the Forest of Dean
Walking in the South Wales
  Valleys
Walking in the Wye Valley
Walking on the Brecon Beacons
Walking on the Gower

For full information on all our
guides, books and eBooks,
visit our website:
www.cicerone.co.uk

Walking – Trekking – Mountaineering – Climbing – Cycling

Over 40 years, Cicerone have built up an outstanding collection of over 300 guides, inspiring all sorts of amazing adventures.

Every guide comes from extensive exploration and research by our expert authors, all with a passion for their subjects. They are frequently praised, endorsed and used by clubs, instructors and outdoor organisations.

All our titles can now be bought as **e-books**, **ePubs** and **Kindle** files and we also have an online magazine – **Cicerone Extra** – with features to help cyclists, climbers, walkers and trekkers choose their next adventure, at home or abroad.

Our website shows any **new information** we've had in since a book was published. Please do let us know if you find anything has changed, so that we can publish the latest details. On our **website** you'll also find great ideas and lots of detailed information about what's inside every guide and you can buy **individual routes** from many of them online.

It's easy to keep in touch with what's going on at Cicerone by getting our monthly **free e-newsletter**, which is full of offers, competitions, up-to-date information and topical articles. You can subscribe on our home page and also follow us on **Facebook** and **Twitter** or dip into our **blog**.

Cicerone – the very best guides for exploring the world.

CICERONE

Juniper House, Murley Moss, Oxenholme Road, Kendal, Cumbria LA9 7RL
Tel: 015395 62069 info@cicerone.co.uk
www.cicerone.co.uk